A Creative Life
God's Design for You

Whitney Von Lake Hopler

Copyright © 2002 by Whitney Von Lake Hopler

A Creative Life
by Whitney Von Lake Hopler

Printed in the United States of America

Library of Congress Control Number: 2002106163
ISBN 1-591600-99-5

All rights reserved. No part of this publication may be reproduced or transmitted in any form or by any means without written permission of the publisher.

Unless otherwise indicated, Bible quotations are taken from The Holy Bible, New International Version. Copyright © 1984 by International Bible Society.

Xulon Press
11350 Random Hills Road
Suite 800
Fairfax, VA 22030
(703) 279-6511
XulonPress.com

To order additional copies, call 1-866-381-BOOK (2665).

Table of Contents

Acknowledgements 7

Introduction 9

Chapter One   God the Creator 13

Chapter Two   Made in God's Image
                                to be Creative............................27

Chapter Three   Exploration 39

Chapter Four   Inspiration 53

Chapter Five   Concentration...67

Chapter Six   Implementation 83

Study Guide   Becoming Fully Creative 97

Acknowledgements

Thanks to God for giving me the ideas contained in this book – and so many more ideas as I seek to live a creative life.

Thanks to my husband Russ for his tireless dedication to this project, encouraging me, reading drafts, discussing ideas, and contributing valuable insights into the creative process.

Thanks to my wonderful daughter Honor, who even at age 4 already inspires me with her creativity.

Thanks to my parents, Jim Wyckoff and Dayna Smith, who have strongly encouraged and supported my writing endeavors since I was a child.

Thanks to editor Marcia McAllister, who gave me my first job in journalism, mentored me in the field, and helped make it possible for me to interview many of the people whose stories fill this book.

Finally, thanks to all my friends, who enrich my life with theirs and whose excitement about a book on creativity has helped motivate me to complete this project.

Introduction

God is creative, but are you? What does it mean to be creative, anyway? Are only certain people creative? Can working on a special project make you creative? Is there any way you can be creative all the time?

Mindy is an at-home mom of an energetic 3-year-old son. Sometimes she feels creative—when she's helping her son paint, build towers with blocks or pound out music on his toy drums. But most often, she feels exhausted and overwhelmed by her daily responsibilities. When she's dealing with yet another tantrum or cleaning up yet another mess, Mindy feels trapped by life's demands and sapped of any creativity she enjoys during some brief, golden moments of playing with her son.

Bill is a computer programmer for a large telecommunications firm. He regularly works long hours, and enjoys the hefty income he receives for his efforts. But lately he's been depressed because, as lucrative as his work is, it bores him. Hour after hour of writing code just doesn't energize him the way composing music does, late at night when he's home alone and can relax with his keyboard and saxophone. No one but Bill himself has ever heard his jazz songs, but it thrills him to tinker with the notes until he creates pieces of music to enjoy. Those are the times that sustain him—the only times when he feels creative.

Keisha thinks of herself as a creative person. After all, she's a graphic designer, and people pay her to be creative. Each time a logo or layout takes form in her head, Keisha is excited about expressing it. Many people have praised her work, and she couldn't be happier with her profession. But Keisha often wishes her personal life would excite her half as much as her job. After just two years of marriage, it seems that the romance has left Keisha's relationship with her husband, and she feels stuck in a rut. Her friends sometimes get on her nerves, and she's not sure why. Her prayer time with God each morning has become more like an obligation than something she truly wants to do.

Now that Stan, a retired plumber, is able to devote time to projects he wants to do—such as restoring an old car in his garage—he feels a lot more creative than when he was working for a paycheck. His granddaughter and some neighborhood kids drop by to visit fairly frequently, and whenever he plays with them, he has a great time. But Stan has to make sure he keeps himself busy, or he'll start to worry. Since his retirement, there's been so much that concerns him. What will he do if his health begins to fail? How will he meet all his expenses with a fixed income? Will his son, to whom he turned over his plumbing company, run the business well, or will customers go elsewhere? Stan doesn't try to seek solutions; he just escapes by pursuing one of his projects to get his mind off everything else.

Mindy, Bill, Keisha and Stan are composites of many people I've known in my work as a journalist. Sometimes they feel creative; sometimes not. They make think they're creative people, or they may yearn for a creativity they don't realize they have. When they're accessing the creativity God has given them, their lives are fulfilling. But often, their

Introduction

lives are limited, because they don't live nearly as creatively as they can. Perhaps you recognize aspects of your life in these examples.

Whether you feel like a creative person or not, you are one. And your creativity doesn't have to be limited to certain times or situations. You can—and should—be creative in all aspects of your life.

The secular view of creativity portrays this God-given gift as a special talent reserved only for people who are artistic, or for children who can afford to have fun before they're shackled by the practical demands of life as adults. But God, the master Creator and source of all creativity, has a far more holistic view. He has created you in his image, and will enable you to participate in his creativity. He wants you to live creatively at all times and in all situations, so your life can become the masterpiece he intends it to be.

Creativity, simply put, is innovative thinking and acting. Everyone can do it, with God's help.

Mankind's fall has affected everything in creation—including people's ability to think and act with the creativity God originally intended. But the good news is that God restores full access to his creative Spirit to those who have a relationship with him through his Son, Jesus Christ.

Jesus said of all who trust him, "... I have come that they may have life, and have it to the full" (John 10:10). Wouldn't it be great to live such an abundant life?

God will make that possible for you if you follow him through the adventure of the creative process. It begins with exploration, in which you seek innovative ideas, then moves to inspiration, when you receive them. The next stage, concentration, involves working on your creative ideas through both thought and action. Finally, implementation entails delivering your ideas to the world and helping others receive them. These different aspects of the creative process sometimes overlap, but this book will examine each stage separately to illustrate the details of how God can guide you through the process.

My fascination with creativity began a few years ago, when I made some major changes in my life. Leaving a job as an editor on staff at a national magazine so I could move to another state with my husband, I wondered if I could ever be very creative without that dream job. But when I became a mom soon afterward and plunged into other activities—including a job working from home—I was glad to discover that my creativity was actually growing. The more I turned to God for creative energy, the more he gave, and the pieces of my life came together in a more holistic and fulfilling way.

It was a rewarding experience to create a Bible study on creativity soon afterward, and lead it with my husband for a group of people at our church. Through that effort, God showed me how deeply people can be encouraged when they pursue more creative lives. Most of the people who participated didn't consider themselves creative at first, but came to discover the richness of their creative gifts and how they could apply them in all aspects of their lives.

Later, I was impressed by how people I interviewed for newspaper stories were using their creativity in a wide variety of ways. You'll meet many of them throughout this book; all the examples I include in the upcoming chapters are true.

This book's purpose is to show you how you can live a more fully creative life as well—no matter what the circumstances of your life are, or whether you've ever previously thought of yourself as creative. It's my prayer that, by the end of this book, you'll discover the uniquely creative life that God has designed for you, and be well on your way toward living it!

CHAPTER ONE

God the Creator

Creativity exists because it is part of God's nature. As God has expressed his creativity, all the elements of our universe have been formed and transformed. God's creative power is boundless, and thinking about it can inspire great awe.

But it can also be intimidating to fathom God's creativity. After all, as creatures, we understand and exercise our creativity within the bounds of limitations that don't constrain God. God doesn't need to depend on anyone, but we must depend on him as the source of our creativity. God can create something from nothing, but when we create something, we must use elements God has already created. All we can do is manage the material God has given us in the universe, so that even our loftiest creations are simply expressions of how we choose to use that God-given material—whether it is matter or ideas. "For by him all things were created: things in heaven and on earth, visible and invisible, whether thrones or powers or rulers or authorities; all things were created by him and for him. He is before all things, and in him all things hold together," declares Col. 1:16-17. God's creative process is also different from ours—unlike us, he doesn't need to explore to discover something new because he knows everything, and he doesn't need to be inspired, because he is the source of all inspiration. God does concentrate on and implement his creative ideas as we do, but perfectly (unlike us!) and sometimes in ways that are different from how we can proceed.

Despite all these differences, however, God's creativity is intimately related to ours. It is through experiencing more of God's creativity that we can live more creative lives.

Knowing the master Creator

God knows us completely—better than we know ourselves. But we can never fit God underneath our microscopes. We can only know what he chooses to reveal about himself—which is often just enough to keep our relationships with him growing. When Moses asked God to describe himself by giving his name, God replied, "'I Am Who I Am'" (Exod. 3:14). God wants us to trust him implicitly, and the qualities he has chosen to reveal about himself show a God who is eminently worthy of that trust.

God has made his mark on every part of his creation, so that many of his characteristics can be discerned from what he has made. "For since the creation of the world, God's invisible qualities—his eternal power and divine nature—have been clearly seen, being understood from what has been made ..." declares Rom. 1:20. When God entered earth's time and space as Jesus Christ, he helped humans understand even more deeply how they can know him. Jesus, says Col. 1:15, "is the image of the invisible God." Through learning about Jesus, we can learn about God the Father. As Jesus himself says in John 14:7, "If you really knew me, you would know my Father as well."

Some aspects of God's character mentioned in the Bible reveal a lot about his creativity. Learning more about those characteristics can help you better understand how they shape God's creation—the environment in which you live and express your own God-given creativity.

God is loving

God's loving nature is the essence of his reason for creating everything. His love motivated him to form creatures to enjoy fellowship with him, and his love permeates his creation, creating a deep communal bond. "God is love," declares 1 John 4:16-17. "Whoever lives in love lives in God, and God in him. In this way, love is made complete among us ... ".

God's creation reflects the boundless depth of his love. "Your love, O Lord, reaches to the heavens, your faithfulness to the skies," says Ps. 36:5. Those who enjoy a relationship with God through Jesus Christ also enjoy the assurance that nothing in all of creation can separate them from God's great love. "For I am convinced that neither death nor life, neither angels nor demons, neither the present nor the future, nor any powers, neither height nor depth, nor anything else in all creation, will be able to separate us from the love of God that is in Christ Jesus our Lord" (Rom. 8:38-39).

God invests great thought and energy into crafting his creation because he loves it so much. He is the ultimate father, loving his children completely. "How great is the love the Father has lavished on us, that we should be called children of God!" (1 John 3:1).

The passionate love that engaged couples share motivates them to create new lives together as married couples. Brian Berry and his fiancée Holly Petty said God's love fueled their passion for each other and gave them the courage to trust God with their future. "God has demonstrated his love for us, and I know he'll give us the grace we'll need for whatever we'll face together," said Berry.

As Berry and Petty prepared for the creative adventure of marriage, they discovered that they could look beyond just their feelings to the steadfast strength of God's love. "A marriage is more about loving another person than being in love with a person," Berry said. "It's an action, not just a feeling." God's love fueled their passion, but it also gave them reliable power to remain committed to the creative work of marriage no matter what circumstances they would face.

Berry and Petty relied on God's love for strength to be creative as they navigated issues during marriage preparation seminars—discussing how they plan to manage their money, who should do what in their future household, whose parents to visit on holidays and more. "I'm excited thinking about getting to share the day-to-day things of life together, but it's very humbling to think that we'll be making decisions that will affect both of us, not just one," said Petty. But, she added, she was confident that God's great love would see them through. "If we really commit ourselves to God, we know he'll have some adventures for us. It's kind of exciting to see what kind of adventures they'll turn out to be."

You, too, can rely on God's love as you seek to live creatively – no matter what situations you face. Many Psalms speak of God's "unfailing" love that "endures forever," and God himself declares in Jer. 31:3, "'I have loved you with an everlasting love ...'". When you tap into that love, you will receive the greatest creative power of all—power that can innovatively transform any situation. "And now these three remain: faith, hope and love. But the greatest of these is love" (1 Cor. 13:13). Let passion motivate you to create new adventures in life, then let God's love sustain you through them.

God is purposeful

God, in his wisdom, gave a purpose to every part of the universe. He designed each part to fulfill a unique function within his master plan. The intricate connections within the earth's ecosystem reflect well-designed purposes—soil, water and sunlight nourish plants, which, in turn, nourish animals, who fertilize the soil with the food waste from their bodies. Everything has a precise purpose, and everything contributes in some way to the greater good of nature in its entirety.

Every one of God's words—creative messages that he sends out—are designed to fulfill his purposes. God says in Isa. 55:11 that his word " ... will not return to me empty, but will accomplish what I desire and achieve the purpose for which I sent it."

While God cares deeply about every part of his creation, he is especially interested in how well we humans fulfill our intended purpose, since he created us in his image and has made us managers of the earth. In John 15:5, Jesus implores his disciples to remain connected to him, so they can fulfill God's purposes in their lives: "I am the vine; you are the branches. If a man remains in me and I in him, he will bear much fruit; apart from me you can do nothing." Fortunately, God will help those who ask him to achieve his purposes. Phil. 2:13 declares, " ... it is God who works in you to will and to act according to his good purpose."

Often, God will masterfully weave the threads of individual lives together to complete the tapestry of his larger purpose in a situation. As Rom. 8:28 declares, " ... we know that in all things God works for the good of those who love him, who have been called according to his purpose."

When I covered a story about a teen and a doctor helping another teen who needed heart surgery, I was inspired by how God's Spirit had brought all three people together to experience his larger purpose working in their lives. Maria Hernandez, 14, had sustained damage to her heart's mitral valve after a bout of rheumatic fever, and was headed for a premature death unless she obtained surgery to repair the valve. But in her home country of Nicaragua, advanced medical care was scarce, and Maria's family couldn't afford it even if it had been available. Living in a hut with a leaking roof, Maria and her brother were supported solely by what their grandmother could earn selling fruit from a basket atop her head. Physician Edward Lefrak, a well-respected cardiac surgeon, met Maria while on a mission trip to Nicaragua that he said God led him to take. Soon he and other medical personnel donated their services to perform the operation free of charge in the United States. Maria recuperated for several weeks with Lefrak's family in their home, and another 14-year-old girl, Lindsay Shore, heard about Maria's operation through news reports. Soon she led a fund-raising drive among her family, friends and fellow church members to obtain money to repair Maria's home in Nicaragua.

God's overarching creative purpose in the situation—that people learn how to love each other each other more deeply—was achieved as all three people learned their own lessons from the experience. Maria learned about the generosity of God and those who love him. Lefrak learned that if he can help even one person, he can make a significant contribution. "It was rewarding to me spiritually; it was a very meaningful experience," he said. "There are thousands of kids in Nicaragua who need heart surgery, so this seems like such a small thing, but at least it's one person we've been able to help, so it's really a big thing." Lindsay learned the joy of giving firsthand. The experience, she said, "has made me more likely to volunteer in the future, because now I know what it's like."

By making themselves available for God to use them, Maria, Lefrak and Lindsay all discovered more about his purposes for their lives. They all three got to participate in adventures that creatively transformed them.

You can be sure that if you commit your creative efforts to God, he will see that their purposes are fulfilled. "Commit to the Lord whatever you do, and your plans will succeed. The Lord works out everything for his own ends ..." says Prov. 16:3-4. In the process, he'll likely transform you as well.

God is infinite

We humans are still discovering the numerous life forms God has created in his vast universe, and the sheer amount of those we already know is mind-boggling. From animals as simple as amoebas and as complex as dolphins to plants as small as a blade of grass and as large as a Redwood tree, God's creative work is truly vast. The aspects of creation described in Neh. 9:6 reveal something of the infiniteness of the One who made them: "You made the heavens, even the highest heavens, and all their starry host, the earth and all that is on it, the seas and all that is in them. You give life to everything, and the multitudes of heaven worship you." Job 26:7-8, 14 marvels at the part of God's creative work that is visible, then exclaims, "And these are but the outer fringe of his works; how faint the whisper we hear of him! Who then can understand the thunder of his power?"

God's thoughts, from which his actions spring, are also infinite. "How precious to me are your thoughts, O God! How vast is the sum of them! Were I to count them, they would outnumber the grains of sand," declares Ps. 139:17-18.

When God led Jim and Janice Narel to raise a large family, he assured them that his support for them would be infinite. The Narels have 10 children—three biological and seven adopted, ranging in age from 29 to 3 years old. Even through 14 moves to follow Jim Narel's career in the U.S. Army—some to other nations such as Korea and Ethiopia—the Narels kept expanding their family, relying on God's infinite provisions for the creative adventure to which he had called them.

"The situation has made us trust in God more than we would have otherwise," said Janice Narel. "It's given us patience and made us humble." She recalled how God's infinite grace helped them care for their youngest child, Erica, after she arrived in their home as a traumatized infant, never crying or smiling as a healthy baby would. "We have lots of arms in here, so we held her a lot, and after a few months, she began to respond," said Janice Narel.

Jim Narel said the sacrifices he and his wife have had to make to fulfill their calling were sometimes challenging, but through it all, God provided everything they needed out of his infinite storehouse of provisions. "Illnesses and behavioral issues and things like that were some issues that we knew we couldn't handle on our own, so we turned to God," he said. "[We've had to] make some financial sacrifices and give up some freedom to travel and spend time together just as spouses. But we wanted to show by our actions what we thought was important. God has given us all we need."

Because the Narels trusted in God's power rather than just their own, they experienced creative abundance instead of frustrating limitations in their lives. They had the wisdom to see possibilities in their dreams, and the courage to act on those dreams, all because they trusted in God's infinite power.

You can trust in God's infinite power to give you all you need for your creative work. "And my God will meet all your needs according to his glorious riches in Christ Jesus" (Phil. 4:19).

God is dynamic

Bubbling up with fiery enthusiasm, bright orange lava poured out of fissures in the ground, darkening to black as it hit the air above. Then waves of water from the nearby Pacific Ocean lapped at the fresh lava, cooling it and shaping it into land. As I stood on that beach on Hawaii's Big Island, I also stood in awe of God. I was witnessing new land being created according to the principles of nature God had set in motion when the earth itself was new. The Big

Island was growing even bigger, thanks to the new land forming every day and expanding its beaches. But Kauai, an older Hawaiian island, was slowly getting smaller as water eroded land on its beaches, a tour guide told our group.

God's dynamic nature is illustrated in his creation, which is constantly transforming. The atomic structure of matter can change; thoughts and prayers can lead to new ideas. God's creation reflects the fact that he is alive and active. "Jesus said to them, `My Father is always at work to this very day, and I, too, am working'" (John 5:17). God's work in the lives of people who choose a relationship with him is so dynamic that it's constantly causing transformation to occur. As 2 Cor. 5:17 declares, "Therefore, if anyone is in Christ, he is a new creation; the old has gone, the new has come!"

When God communicates with his creatures, he changes the ways he delivers his messages according to how he knows the intended recipients will best understand those messages. Sometimes he uses angels as his messengers; other times he speaks directly through his Holy Spirit to a person's spirit. He can speak through Scripture, or through a dream. He can use symbols or circumstances to get his points across.

A mostly African-American congregation working with a mostly Caucasian congregation on community service projects in their town created a better community because they valued the dynamic nature of diversity among people. The churches' members worked together on projects that included repairing local houses and traveling on mission trips. They participated in Bible studies together; they sometimes worshipped together. But rather than try to ignore their differences, they embraced them, and through that, they experienced God's creativity working in their lives.

"There's a sense by some that they want a color-blind society, that everyone should be the same. But we need to celebrate and embrace our differences and what we can each contribute to the mix," said Rev. Kenny Smith, pastor of the mostly African-American church. "God made us distinct for a purpose—he doesn't want us all to be the same. He wants us to learn from each other."

Establishing relationships with people who are different in some way—such as through race, gender, temperament or economic status—helps people discover new ways of experiencing the same God through Christ. Every person you meet changes you, because he or she enlarges your perspective and broadens your life experiences. "Learn each other's stories; share each other's faith journeys," said Robert Griffin, associate pastor of the mostly Caucasian congregation. "Begin to understand and appreciate the diversity within the unity we have in Christ."

Change—which is essential for creativity—is a vital part of God's great design. Although change is a natural part of how our world works, all too often, we respond to it in fear—fear of a future unknown to us, fear of losing a sense of security that we have wrongly tied to the creation rather than the Creator. Remembering that God—who never changes—is in control of the constant change you experience will help you embrace that change as a sign of his work in your life. Christ, says Col. 1:16-17, is the glue that holds the universe together. "For by him all things were created: things in heaven and on earth, visible and invisible ... all things were created by him and for him. He is before all things, and in him all things hold together."

God is emotional

God isn't a remote, unfeeling being who has distanced himself from his creation. He cares deeply about his creative work and is intimately involved with it, expressing a wide range of emotions as he expresses his creativity.

After creating the universe, God showed his pleasure in it by pronouncing it "very good" (Gen. 1:31). But when sin

God the Creator

entered the world and marred his creation, God was deeply saddened. He allowed Adam and Eve—who had brought about that sin by disobeying God—to experience pain, such as through childbirth (Gen. 3:19) and toil while struggling to produce food (Gen. 3:17). He made them vulnerable to death " ... for dust you are and to dust you will return" (Gen. 3:19). Then he banished them from the Garden of Eden (Gen.3:23).

Sin began to permeate God's creation, and by the time of Noah, "The Lord was grieved that he had made man on the earth, and his heart was filled with pain," (Gen. 6:5). Motivated by that pain, God decided to undertake a creative act of destruction, wiping out every living creature except for the faithful Noah, his family, and the creatures on the ark, who repopulated the earth after the flood waters receded. But Noah's faithful worship after he left the ark moved God to promise never to destroy earth's life again. After Noah built an altar and sacrificed burnt offerings on it, "The Lord smelled the pleasing aroma and said in his heart: Never again will I curse the ground because of man, even though every inclination of his heart is evil from childhood. And never again will I destroy all living creatures, as I have done" (Gen. 8:20-21).

For many generations, God continued to express his emotions as he communicated with his creatures, graciously helping those who trusted him by providing all they needed and lashing out with righteous anger at those who rebelled. Then, at the time he had planned, God entered his own creation as Jesus Christ to reconcile it to himself. His compassion motivated him to reach down into his creation in the most intimate way possible—by doing for his creatures what they couldn't do for themselves. In the ultimate act of creativity, God sent his own Son to take the punishment for human sin and free people from its grasp. "For God was pleased to have all his fullness dwell in him [Jesus], and through him to reconcile to himself all things, whether things on earth or things in heaven, by making peace through his blood, shed on the cross" declares Col. 1:19-20.

Jesus experienced the full range of emotions that we humans do, since he was fully human as well as fully divine. After his friend Lazarus died, Jesus wept tears of sadness (John 11:35). He surely experienced joy as he blessed a crowd of children (Mark 10:16) and celebrated at a wedding feast (John 2:1-11). In fact, Jesus performed a great creative act – his first public miracle – by changing water into wine at that wedding, because he felt a strong desire to help the hosts who had run out of wine. Jesus' anger at seeing people use a temple as a marketplace led him to drive animals out with a whip and overturn the tables of the people who were selling them (John 2:15). He experienced the sting of temptation when he encountered Satan in the wilderness (Matt. 4:1-11). After his resurrection, he enjoyed a peaceful breakfast with some friends (John 21:9-13).

After Jesus ascended to heaven, God sent his Holy Spirit to those who put their faith in him. God continues to express himself by living inside some of his creatures—people who are connected to him through Jesus—in the form of the Holy Spirit, jealously longing for their full attention (James 4:5) and grieving if they sin (Eph. 4:30). He also expresses his patience and hopefulness as he deals with creatures who are separated from him: "He is patient with you, not wanting anyone to perish, but everyone to come to repentance" (2 Pet. 3:9).

Since God cares deeply about his creation, he cares very much about you as one of his creatures. He has given you your emotions, and they can be powerful tools to motivate you to pursue creative efforts. So pay attention to your feelings, and let them draw you into creative pursuits as God leads. God yearns for you to care deeply about your creative efforts so that you will fully invest yourself in them, just as

He does.

As you pursue your creative work, remember that, "The Lord your God is with you, he is mighty to save. He will take great delight in you, he will quiet you with his love, he will rejoice over you with singing" (Zep. 3:17).

CHAPTER TWO

Made in God's Image to be Creative

Since God has created you in his image, his creative power flows through you. "For in him [God] we live and move and have our being" (Acts 17:28). God will enable you to participate in his creativity. And not only can you be creative, but you should be, since God strongly desires all his people to use their creativity. God began encouraging people to be creative soon after he created the very first human, Adam, by asking Adam to name the animals he had created. "He brought them to the man to see what he would name them; and whatever the man called each living creature, that was its name" (Gen. 2:19). Deep within us, God has placed a drive to be creative. We instinctively yearn to transcend the limits of our own selves, and in that yearning we reach out for God's creativity and participate in it. God created us out his love, and we create out of the love he has made an integral part of us.

Creatures meant to create

God has given humans the exquisite honor and awesome responsibility of managing his creation on earth. "O Lord, our Lord, how majestic is your name in all the earth! ... When I consider the heavens, the work of your fingers ... what is man that you are mindful of him...? You made him ruler over the works of your hands; you put everything under his feet" (Ps. 8:1, 3-4, 6.). God has also given humans the eminently important task of spreading the message of his plan to redeem our fallen world. "And he has committed to us the message of reconciliation. We are therefore Christ's ambassadors, as though God were making his appeal through us" (2 Cor. 5:19-20). In his vision of the redeemed creation in the future, the apostle John saw creatures singing to Christ about how humans will reign with God. "' ... with your blood you purchased men for God from every tribe and language and people and nation. You have made them to be a kingdom and priests to serve our God, and they will reign on the earth'" (Rev. 5:9-10).

The charge to share in God's creative power as his appointed servants is a wonderful privilege, but, unfortunately, one that is not always fulfilled well. Since caretakers must be healthy themselves before they can serve effectively, God wants you to pursue good holistic health so you can contribute well to the creation you manage. You can prepare yourself to live a more creative life through spiritual, mental and physical practices that form a solid foundation from which to pursue creativity. These three areas of health are intertwined, as Scripture illustrates: "Therefore I urge you, brothers, in view of God's mercy, to offer your *bodies* as living sacrifices, holy and pleasing to God—this is your *spiritual* act of worship. Do not conform any longer to the pattern of this world, but be transformed by the renewing of your *mind*" (Rom. 12:1-2, italics added for emphasis).

As you pursue a holistically healthy life, you will grow closer to God, and that strong relationship with him will, in turn, enable you to continue to grow even healthier. God likens himself to a potter and humans to clay when he asks the rhetorical question, "Does the clay say to the potter, 'What are you making?'" in Isa. 45:9. His message is clear—he wants to mold your life, and every part of it.

So think of your life as a fertile field that has great potential to bear creative fruit, and heed the advice in Hos. 10:12, "Sow for yourselves righteousness, reap the fruit of unfailing love, and break up your unplowed ground; for it is time to seek the Lord until he comes and showers righteousness on you."

Building creativity through spiritual intimacy

Each morning before we get too far into our day, my husband Russ and I take a few minutes to pray. We haven't missed a morning during our nearly seven years of marriage so far—despite business trips that separate us (we pray on the phone), busyness that distracts us (we ignore the pressing demands long enough to pray) and hurt feelings that sap our motivation (we pray anyway, knowing that God will meet us even in—sometimes especially in—anger or sadness). Building spiritual intimacy with God enables us to meet each situation we encounter with much greater creativity than would otherwise be possible. After prayer, we're better able to explore, discover God's inspiration, concentrate on innovative ideas and implement them. Prayer is the means through which we can receive the creative power in God's Holy Spirit poured into our spirits. Numerous times, God has given me creative ideas while praying our morning devotions, and just as frequently, he has used that prayer time to send me the strength I need to help me through the process of pursuing a creative effort.

Prayer is the way to start preparing yourself to live a more creative life. If you set aside a regular time for prayer each day—perhaps in the evening just before bed or at lunchtime if the morning isn't a good time for you—you'll build the discipline necessary to establish a regular connection to

God, the source of all creativity. In the process, you'll likely find yourself adding prayers throughout the day, because your relationship with God will grow deeper and you'll want to talk with him more and more. The classic "ACTS" prayer format can help you foster a deeper relationship with God rather than just asking him to meet your needs and desires. It includes adoration (praising God for who he is), confession (confessing your sins to him), thanksgiving (thanking him for how he has worked in your life and the lives of others you know) and supplication (presenting requests to him). Be sure to also include some time for silence, asking God to use that time to speak to your spirit with whatever he wants to say to you.

Regular Bible reading is also imperative for building the spiritual intimacy that promotes creativity. "All Scripture is God-breathed and is useful for teaching, rebuking, correcting and training in righteousness, so that the man of God may be thoroughly equipped for every good work" (2 Tim. 3:16-17). Since God often speaks through his Word, be sure to read your Bible frequently, praying that God will make the words come alive for you and speak directly to where you are in your life's journey. This will also increase your awareness that God loves you and has confidence in you. It will help you overcome insecurity and tackle the creative projects you sense God calling you to undertake.

Participating weekly in a church is another basic way to build spiritual intimacy that too many people ignore, much to their detriment. Believing in Christ is only part of the equation that results in a fruitful relationship with him. The other vital part is acting on that faith—living it out within the body of Christ. The fellowship of others through church is essential because it provides the guidance, accountability, encouragement, and support everyone needs to grow in their relationships with God. There is also more power to people's divinely lit creative sparks when they're around each other—the sparks can more easily ignite into powerful flames. "And let us consider how we may spur one another on toward love and good deeds. Let us not give up meeting together, as some are in the habit of doing, but let us encourage one another ... " (Heb. 10:24-25).

You can also build spiritual intimacy that fosters creativity by making your activities sacramental—inviting God to meet you there, and preparing to encounter him with reverence and gratitude. A regular activity in many churches—communion—is my favorite formal sacrament, because it makes the spiritual reality of what Christ did for the world on the cross powerfully tangible to me in physical form. Communion, baptism and other ceremonial activities accomplish special purposes in God's church. But you can invite God to meet you in any moment of your life by acknowledging his presence with you and thanking him for who he is and the gift of that particular moment. This practice will dramatically increase your awareness of how to use the senses God has given you, and thereby heighten your creativity.

Invite God to meet you in your everyday experiences, and you'll notice how close he is to you. Each time you use one of your senses (seeing, hearing, smelling, touching and tasting), pray for a sense of God's presence with you in that moment, and your life can be filled with sacramental experiences. Consider how each sight, sound, smell, feeling and flavor reminds you of the master creator: sights such as the radiance of the sun reflecting off the metallic silver paint of a car or an intriguing expression on the face of a person who walks past you, sounds like the rumble of construction equipment or the jittery chirp of a bird, smells such as the pungent odor of freshly cut grass or the sweet aroma of your favorite soap, feelings like the softness of your child's hair or the smooth coolness of a floor you walk across barefoot in the winter and flavors such as the tangy zing of a lemon and the buttery warmth of a freshly baked biscuit.

When you take a sacramental approach to life, you become aware of the value of each moment, and more fully understand the importance of consecrating each moment of your life to God. God cares about each moment of your life, even if it doesn't seem particularly significant to you on the surface. Participants in a ministry devoted to helping people find new jobs said they discovered that God was powerfully at work in their lives during times they at first saw as unproductive. As they prepared for creative transitions from unemployment to employment or one job to another, they tried to build spiritual intimacy with God.

Before they could effectively go through the creative process of exploring new job ideas, receiving inspiration about jobs, concentrating on pursuing new jobs or implementing job changes in their lives, they first needed to focus on spiritual growth. "A job is an important part of your life," said Christian Stallsmith, who signed up for the program after moving from another state. "But it's just one part of your life, and the most important thing is getting right with God in all areas of your life so you can be doing what he's called you to do."

Ministry founder Jack Dunlap emphasized the importance of spiritual growth for all people preparing for job transitions through the program. "We want to help people find God's plan for their lives; we want people to use this time to learn and grow," he said. "We want people to discover a real functional relationship with God, where they can say, `I trust you, Lord.' The way we count our success is when someone comes up to us and says, `I got my life right with God during this time. I used the time not for spiritual depletion, but for spiritual renewal.' And they may have gotten a job, but maybe not. Many of them, of course, do find jobs, but that's a secondary benefit. The primary benefit is the spiritual growth."

Ministry participant Darlene Dolbey recalled how she

grew from being "very depressed" when she first joined the program to a place of security rooted in a close relationship with God. Dolbey had previously gone through a long string of jobs—marketer, data entry worker, beautician, waitress—before finding herself unemployed and in a financial crisis. "I had done everything I knew how to do to support myself, but didn't know what my purpose was," she said.

The prayers of others in the program helped Dolbey prepare for whatever creative changes God would choose to make in her life by encouraging her to build spiritual intimacy with him. "After they prayed for me, I began to get a sense of direction, so I've been able to realize that I'm put here for a reason, that God values me," she said.

In the process, Dolbey got another job to help pay her bills—working on local politicians' campaigns—but hadn't yet acquired a long-term job that she would consider part of a career. Still, Dolbey said, the spiritual work she'd been pursuing prepared her well for the future. "I'm not depressed anymore," she said, "because I know that I can trust the Lord to provide. And he's shown me where I fit in the scheme of things by guiding me gradually, day by day."

Building creativity through mental attitudes

Imagine what it's like to be on vacation. Each day you anticipate discovering new adventures. You relax more than you usually do; you notice more in your environment than you usually do. You use your senses to experience new things, and record memorable moments for posterity. Many of the attitudes people adopt while on vacation help foster creativity. Whether or not you're on a trip, however, you can prepare yourself for creative journeys by putting a little vacation in every day. Don't think of any day as an ordinary one; instead, think of each day as an extraordinary gift from God that's meant to be lived to the fullest. As Ps. 118:24 proclaims in a well-known passage, "This is the day the

Lord has made; let us rejoice and be glad in it." Even on days when sorrow seems nearer than gladness, each day has a purpose in your life: " ... inwardly we are being renewed day by day" (2 Cor. 4:16).

Preparing yourself for creative journeys also involves eliminating clutter from your life—things that sap your resources such as time and energy, but don't help you be more creative. People who practiced a lifestyle called voluntary simplicity shared how the attitudes they adopted freed them to focus on what they considered to be truly important. The lives of many other people around them seemed to be choreographed to beat of voices declaring, "more, more, more!" But those who pursued voluntary simplicity escaped the demands of hectic, complicated schedules and the waste of out-of-control consumerism and debt. By paring down their lives to what mattered most to them, they discovered greater meaning in life and more innovative ideas to consider. And because they had stripped away clutter from their lives, they were able to effectively pursue those creative ideas.

"A lot of people are finding that following the `more is better' message in our culture isn't ultimately fulfilling," said Peter Kelsey, founder of an organization that helps people study voluntary simplicity and other related topics. "Big houses and new cars only bring transitory happiness. When we live simply, we can cut through the distractions that rob us of time, so we're able to decide on and invest in our values for true happiness. A lot of people are exploring voluntary simplicity as a way of creating more time to focus on what's meaningful to them."

Study group participant Beth Braxton said embracing an attitude of simplicity helped her appreciate the creativity in everyday activities. "When we're buying into the fast-paced consumerism that says we've got to do more and acquire more, there's a point we reach at which our lives no longer have much meaning or integrity anymore," she said. "Life is, at its roots, basic and simple. True happiness comes from things like sharing the joy of a conversation with a friend or watching a cardinal out on a birdfeeder."

Study group leader Jack Davis had made many sacrifices to simplify his life—passing up lucrative jobs in favor of more meaningful volunteer work, repairing items rather than buying new ones, carving out time to make food like bread from scratch rather than consume processed food. But the greatest reward of pursuing his creative ideas—freedom—far outweighed the sacrifices, he said. "The most profound change that comes to those who successfully adjust to a simpler life is a sense of freedom," said Davis, adding that the freedom he experienced included freedom, "from wanting an endless flow of things and possessions that must be replaced with even grander and expensive stuff. Freedom to pursue a more relaxed and slower life. Freedom to seriously consider changing careers and doing something you love rather than what is required to buy what a materialistic society makes you think you need."

You can declare yourself on vacation from a life that doesn't foster your creativity. By adopting attitudes of curiosity, awe and wonder, you can prepare yourself well for a richer creative journey. By putting aside fear and doubt and embracing courage and faith, you can discover whatever new creative adventures God has planned for you. Make Eph. 4:23 your prayer as you strive to align your mental attitudes with the ones God wants you to adopt for maximum creativity: " ... put off your old self, which is being corrupted by its sinful desires; to be made new in the attitude of your minds; and ... put on the new self, created to be like God in true righteousness and holiness."

Building creativity through physical care

Your body contains many tools to help you live creatively—your eyes, ears, nose, skin and tongue help you explore your environment; your brain helps you receive new ideas and concentrate on them; your hands and feet help you implement creative ideas. If you neglect your body's care, your creativity will be hindered. Simply recalling a time when you've been sick will give you a good picture of how limited your life can be when your body isn't functioning as it should. If you take good care of your body, however, you increase the chances that it will function well, enabling you to reach more of your creative potential.

The source of creativity—God himself—lives inside the bodies Christians in the form the Holy Spirit. "Do you not know that your body is a temple of the Holy Spirit, who is in you, whom you have received from God? You are not your own; you were bought at a price. Therefore honor God with your body" (1 Cor. 6:19-20).

Since God has designed human bodies, it makes sense to turn to him for guidance on how to take care of them, said people trying to lose weight through a biblically based program. "God designed our bodies with hunger signals that are uniquely set for each person," said Ginni Richards, who coordinated the weight loss program at her church and emphasized how participants should eat whenever they were hungry, but only then, and only as much food as it took to make them feel full.

God has programmed your body to transmit signals about many of its needs. If you're tired, your body needs sleep. If your arm hurts, the pain may be alerting you to a physical problem. Paying attention to those signals and responding well to them helps you build habits of listening that will be invaluable in your creative process. Program participant Susie Massa said pursuing better physical health helped her draw closer to God, freeing her to fulfill more of his creative purposes for her life. "As I brought my eating under control, a lot of other areas in my life improved because I could see how God was calling me to live," she said. "When we're in a right relationship with God, we can become more and more like the people he created us to be."

The principles of taking good care of your physical health are fairly simple—maintain a consistent sleep schedule, exercise regularly, eat lots of fruits and vegetables, avoid cigarettes—it's all basically common sense. What's more complicated and challenging is trying to apply those principles to your life. God will meet you at your point of need, though, and shepherd you through the process of taking care of your body. Incorporating changes into your life—such as eating small meals frequently throughout the day rather than a few large ones, or going to bed each night an hour earlier than you had before—will likely be tough at first, but then become a natural part of your lifestyle if you incorporate them gradually and rely on God's grace as you do.

If you keep your body as fit as possible, you'll sharpen your mind and spirit as well, since all three parts of you are interconnected. So each time you take care of your body, you'll find you're on your way toward a more creative life.

Getting ready for adventure

Once you've prepared yourself spiritually, mentally and physically to live a healthier life, you're ready to take stock of the unique gifts God has bestowed on you and consider how you might use them more creatively. "We have different gifts, according to the grace given us," declares Rom. 12:6, before listing examples of spiritual gifts—prophesying, serving, teaching, encouraging, giving, leading and showing mercy. In addition to your unique spiritual gifts, you also have distinctive mental and physical gifts you can draw upon as you seek to live a more creative life. Do you have good analytical skills or a witty sense of humor? Are you able to figure out mechanical details when others are stumped by how to build or repair something? Do you consider yourself a graceful person with a good kinesthetic sense? Does your stamina help you persevere when others get tired? God has a purpose for each of your unique gifts. When you're aware of what they are, you can seek to use them well during the creative process.

God wants you to be resourceful, using your gifts to the fullest. He'll be pleased if you invest your gifts well, and disappointed if you don't. Jesus' parables of the talents in Matt. 25:14-30 and the ten minas in Luke 19:12-27 illustrate how God intends for his people to be creative as they use their gifts, and shows how he responds according to what they choose to do. In the parable of the talents, a man going on a trip entrusted three servants with money. When he returns to discover that two of them invested the money—using it creatively—he praises each one, saying, "Well done, good and faithful servant! You have been faithful with a few things; I will put you in charge of many things. Come and share your master's happiness!" (Matt. 25:21,23). When he hears that the third servant merely hid his money in the ground because he was afraid to do anything creative with it, however, the man lashes out angrily at him. "His master replied, `You wicked, lazy servant! ... you should have put my money on deposit with the bankers, so that when I returned I would have received it back with interest.'" (Matt. 25:26-27). Then the master instructs others to take the third servant's money and give it to a servant who invested his money well.

If you have prepared yourself well to use your creativity, you'll be able to fulfill the commission God has given you to be creative, and grow closer to him while doing so. Strive to, "Be dressed ready for service and keep your lamps burning ... " like the men Jesus describes in his story in Luke 12:35, alluding to his second coming. Live your life in a state of readiness for whatever adventures God plans to bring your way.

CHAPTER THREE

Exploration

The creative process begins with exploration, and there is so much to explore! God is waiting to reveal innumerable potential new ideas to those who seek them out. As the source of all that's exciting to discover, God invites you to search for him so he can show you a more creative life. "'You will seek me and find me when you seek me with all your heart. I will be found by you,' declares the Lord" (Jer. 29:13-14). Ps. 34:10 reveals that, "Those who seek the Lord lack no good thing."

Becoming an explorer

Lurching over grocery bags splayed out across the kitchen floor, I grabbed a can of peas just before my infant daughter Honor had a chance to lift its shiny lid up to her mouth. "No, sweetie, there are germs there," I said, as her cries of disappointment filled the air. Then, as I reached for a toy to replace the can, I stumbled backward, bumping my arm on a counter.

The shrill ring of a telephone drew my attention away from the pain in my arm, and after answering it I heard the excited voice of my sister Courtney, a U.S. Marine Corps public affairs officer who was then stationed in Japan. "Hey guess what?" she said. "I'm calling from the summit of Mount Fuji right now! The view is great. Wish you could be here to see it!"

"So do I," I said, a bit too desperately. "What does it look like?"

"Well," Courtney said, "the sky is full of color. It's sunrise here. We hiked for hours during the night, but it was worth it."

After a brief conversation, I transferred the phone to my mom and sank down dejectedly into a chair. My schedule that day—driving my mom to the grocery store and a doctor's appointment, taking care of Honor, and trying to cram in some writing before a looming deadline—just didn't come close to the excitement of climbing a beautiful mountain in a faraway place. Actually, I would've been thrilled to take a trip anywhere—even to a local park—to escape the mundane demands of my life.

Do you ever fantasize about what it would be like to be an explorer? Some people can afford the time and money to scout wild animals in Kenya, navigate the Amazon River or snowshoe in Norway. But many can't, and even those who can take some exciting trips aren't able to spend every day living so dramatically.

The good news is that we can all be explorers—right where we are, right now. "Ask and it will be given to you; seek and you will find; knock and the door will be opened to you. For everyone who asks receives; he who seeks finds; and to him who knocks, the door will be opened" (Matt. 7:7). As we cultivate a sense of exploration in our everyday living, God will send us many sparks to ignite our creativity.

Developing a sense of wonder

Children know this. Unencumbered by pretentiousness and cynicism—qualities that can creep into adult hearts weary from living in this fallen world—children embody the sense of wonder that Jesus wants all of us to have. Jesus said in Matt. 18:3, "'I tell you the truth, unless you change and become like little children, you will never enter the kingdom of heaven.'" Children are humble enough to be explorers, because they're conscious of how much they depend on others and therefore need to trust in the world around them rather than in themselves alone. And children get excited about exploring their world because they believe they'll make exciting new discoveries if they just make the effort to explore.

I do have to admit that a shiny lid on a can of peas doesn't fascinate me nearly as much as it does my daughter. Nor do I expect that any adult would be enthralled by studying groceries, even though young children might be. It is true that children, who have limited experiences so far in their lives, encounter more that is new to them in life than adults do. The sheer novelty of these experiences encourages more exploration.

But as adults, we can choose to share in the same attitude children have—a constant sense of wonder—as we go through each day. Eccles. 5:7 urges, "... stand in awe of God."

We're always encountering new situations in our lives; reminding ourselves that God is in control of them instills a healthy sense of reverence for him. And there are many new details to notice about people, places or things that are already familiar to us; wondering about them will lead us to some intriguing discoveries.

If you develop a sense of wonder, you'll start to recognize the wonderful riches that await explorers!

Relinquishing the status quo

It can often seem a lot less taxing to maintain the status quo in your life's circumstances than to explore other options. People tend to resist change, because change is often downright uncomfortable. But life has a way of bringing change to us, since change is an integral part of God's plan for our lives. He intended us to be dynamic beings living in a dynamic world. Jesus' parable in Luke 5:36-39 about the futility of patching an old garment with new cloth and pouring new wine into old wineskins illustrates how he intends us to leave the past behind so we can move freely into new chapters of our lives.

Sometimes life enforces change upon us. Corporate downsizing can make finding a new job a necessity rather than a choice. An unexpected pregnancy can cause a husband and wife to rewrite their future plans. Many times, though, we'll sense that a change is in order, but refuse to pursue it, because we're afraid of how our lives might be different if we do. Someone offered a chance to visit a third world country she'd always been fascinated with might decline to take the trip because seeing people in dire need would upset her and compel her to make financial sacrifices to help. A person asked to coach his son's soccer team might be reluctant to commit to the job despite wanting to support his son more, for fear that the practice and game schedule would consume all his free time.

When we surrender our ideas to fear—the opposite of faith—we're drawing our security from the circumstances in our lives that make us comfortable. But God is the only true source of our security. Jesus' disciples knew that, and acted on that faith when he first called them. Matthew 4:18-22 records that Peter, Andrew, James and John were all going about their work as fishermen when Jesus walked along the Sea of Galilee and asked them to follow him. They responded immediately, setting aside everything else.

There is no safer place to be than in the center of God's will for your life. That doesn't mean you'll be immune to the pain that change can sometimes bring. But it does mean you'll be free of the dangers of situations that God doesn't intend for you—circumstances that he knows will inhibit your growth and prevent you from becoming the person he wants you to be. God's plan for your life isn't the easiest one, but it definitely is the most rewarding option.

So pray for the strength to relinquish any hold you might have on the status quo in your life. If you sense God leading you to explore a new idea, you can count on him to be right beside you every step of the way as you pursue it. "Be strong and courageous. Do not be afraid ... for the Lord your God goes with you; he will never leave you nor forsake you" (Deut. 31:6).

Embracing forgiveness

Stepping into the future means leaving the past behind. You may yearn to relinquish status quo circumstances in your life, but be unable to truly move beyond them if you're harboring resentment toward someone who has hurt you in the past. That's why embracing forgiveness is vitally important to becoming an explorer.

Willie Williams, resident of a Christian rehabilitation center for alcohol and drug addicts, described how he experienced the searing burns of hate when some inmates at a prison where he was incarcerated threw gasoline on his face and lit it. His face was badly and permanently scarred. But his spirit was unscathed, because he had chosen to forgive the men who hurt him. Forgiveness wasn't something Williams was able to offer from his own strength, but when he began a relationship with God at the rehabilitation center, he prayed for God's grace to enable him to forgive. That same power from God also helped Williams kick his addictions to heroin and alcohol, and even overcome his fear of fire. Shortly after our interview, he lit candles during an Advent worship service to thank God for the warm flame of hope he had kindled in him.

"I have no animosity with anyone today," Williams said. "My heart is clean." With his new heart, Williams is able to explore a life completely different from the one he had previously lived for 40 years, shuttling in and out of various prisons since childhood. "This is a new experience for me—doing right," he said. "And sometimes I get scared by all the responsibility. But I'm taking it one day at a time and the Lord is helping me."

Forgiving others releases God's forgiveness for you as well; refusing to forgive blocks God's forgiveness in your life. "For if you forgive men when they sin against you, your heavenly Father will also forgive you. But if you do not forgive men their sins, your Father will not forgive your sins" (Matt. 6:14-15). Bitterness hinders the creative process because it clouds your mind and blocks your intimacy with God, the source of creativity. But forgiveness opens the way for you to discover a more creative life.

Finding the "right" way to do things

Have you ever wondered whether there might be a better way to do things than the "right" way—the way things have traditionally been done, or the way others expect you to do them?

A business manager might decide to run his department according to how it has been operated for years, despite a gnawing sense that he should introduce a new plan to help faltering sales. Newlyweds might argue over whose parents to visit for Christmas, with a cloud of hurt feelings from in-laws hanging over them.

The pressure you can experience from going against an expected course of action can be tremendous. When my husband Russ and I decided—after months of intense prayer, thought and counsel—to have just one child, God gave us his peace that one child was right for our family, for many reasons. But American culture prescribes two children for each couple. Those who have less, like us, and those who have more, like a friend of mine with four children, are constantly asked to explain their decisions as if

Exploration

they are somehow wrong.

Throughout history, many people have unfortunately ignored God's leading to bow to the whims of others. Jesus was upset with the Pharisees for paying more attention to traditions rather than God's will. "'You have let go of the commands of God and are holding on to the traditions of men,'" he said in Mark 7:8.

As an explorer, you need to ask yourself the fundamental question, "What does God want me to do?" in every situation, and train yourself to listen for his voice rising above the cacophony of other voices. God will give you the strength you need to do it.

Placing margins in your life

It's typically in the margins that people take notes. As an explorer, it's important to create margins on the pages of your life, so you'll have room to incorporate the discoveries you make. That means carving out some free time from your schedule on a regular basis. Busyness that crowds out God's voice and exhausts people is an epidemic problem in our society today. God has designed a natural rhythm for living, and aligning your life with that design will help enable you to live it well.

Placing boundaries on the various activities in your schedule will keep them from seeping into times you could be exploring. And taking a day to worship and rest each week—the Sabbath day God has commanded—will give you the renewed energy you need for the other six days of the week. Most people choose to make Sunday their Sabbath day, but for those who cannot (doctors on call, for example), another day, such as Saturday, can work.

If you haven't yet practiced keeping the Sabbath, you might imagine you'd be bored silly from resting for an entire day. But a Sabbath day can be as active as all the other days of your week, just in a different kind of way. Free from the distractions of other tasks that usually consume your attention, you're able to explore more of what God wants you to notice, and the discoveries you make can energize you as much as if you were a battery being recharged. Making time for worship enables you to encounter God in a fresh way and learn more about him from the experience. "There remains, then, a Sabbath-rest for the people of God; for anyone who enters God's rest also rests from his own work, just as God did from his. Let us, therefore, make every effort to enter that rest ... " exhorts Heb. 4:9-11.

Listening enthusiastically

Explorers relish the potential new discoveries awaiting them. An athlete figuring out how hard his body will work as he plays his favorite sport, a salesperson seizing opportunities before they're lost, a patient with a rare disease researching the best treatment plan—they all have an intense drive to explore.

That enthusiasm is the kind of attitude God wants explorers to have. No matter what your circumstances, if you listen eagerly for God's voice, he will likely reward your effort with discoveries only he can provide. When the prophet Samuel told God, "Speak, for your servant is listening," God replied, "See, I am about to do something in Israel that will make the ears of everyone who hears of it tingle" (1 Sam. 3:10-11). Jesus promised to commune with those who listen for and respond to his voice. "Here I am! I stand at the door and knock. If anyone hears my voice and opens the door, I will come in and eat with him, and he with me" (Rev. 3:20).

Listening for God's voice is always an adventure. Often, it's not immediately apparent; sometimes it takes an excruciatingly long time to hear. But committing yourself to prayer when you're searching for creative ideas will reap rewards from God's Holy Spirit at the right time. "I keep asking that the God of our Lord Jesus Christ, the glorious

Father, may give you the Spirit of wisdom and revelation, so that you may know him better," wrote the apostle Paul. "I pray also that the eyes of your heart may be enlightened in order that you may know the hope to which he has called you, the riches of his glorious inheritance in the saints, and his incomparably great power for us who believe" (Eph. 1:17-19).

It may seem more natural to seek out God's ideas when you're facing major decisions, such as whether to move or to marry a certain person. Sometimes, you may want to ask God for guidance for other choices as well—choices that aren't necessarily life-altering, but still important to you—like deciding whether to invest in a certain mutual fund or choosing how to celebrate your child's high school graduation. But what about all those other decisions you face throughout each day, or those times when you're not facing a decision that must be made?

Don't hesitate to ask God for guidance about anything, no matter how small it may seem. And don't neglect listening for his voice even when you're not seeking help with a particular decision. It's incredible, but true: God is interested in every detail of your life. "And even the very hairs of your head are all numbered" (Matt. 10:30). The riches to which God can lead you in every situation are the treasures you should seek as an explorer. By seeking God's voice continuously, you'll discover much more than if you seek it infrequently. And best of all, you'll foster a deeper relationship with the one who created all there is to explore.

There are many gems for you to find as an explorer by listening to other people, as well. But listening isn't the same as merely hearing words. It's not a passive activity; it's an active pursuit that requires giving your full attention to what others say. As Solomon says in Prov. 5:1, " ... pay attention to my wisdom, listen well to my words of insight ... ".

Start by asking questions whenever you're curious about

something. Make it a regular practice to ask most people you encounter during each day at least one question. Then strive to focus completely whenever anyone is talking to you, shutting out distractions. While other people are talking to you, how often have you been forming judgments about what they're saying, or rehearsing what you would like to say in response? Once they've stopped talking, are you able to repeat back to them what you understood them to say? It may take awhile to train yourself to focus entirely on what others say while they're speaking, but the effort will yield riches for you as an explorer. Listening to others with an ear for things you have never done before can prove particularly intriguing and rewarding.

Trying new things

Each day brings with it a myriad of opportunities to try something new. As you seize those opportunities, you cultivate a lifestyle of exploration. Cooking a meal you've never tried before, driving a new route to work, buying a CD of jazz music when you usually listen to rock—the list of new things you can try is literally endless. Be proactive in your quest for new experiences.

When you encounter opportunities to try something new, be courageous! Remember that God will do something exciting if you obey His nudges to step into something you haven't experienced before. It's so easy to listen to the voices of doubt that can crowd out His Spirit in your mind – voices that tell you it won't be worth the effort to risk a new pursuit. But consider what happened when Jesus' disciples decided to heed His words when he appeared to them by the Sea of Tiberias after His resurrection. The disciples had spent the previous night trying to catch some fish, to no avail. Once Jesus appeared in the early morning and suggested that they try fishing in a new place, however, they decided to go for it. What happened next was an explorer's dream – they discovered treasure beyond what they had expected! "He called to them, 'Friends, haven't you any fish?' 'No,' they answered. He said, 'Throw your net on the right side of the boat and you will find some.' When they did, they were unable to haul the net in because of the large number of fish" (John 21:5-6).

As you pursue something new, think about how that experience helps enlarge your mind and spirit. Pray about how God can use it to draw you closer to him. In Jer. 33:3, God says, "'Call to me and I will answer you and tell you great and unsearchable things you do not know.'"

Looking for potential

Every situation you encounter contains greater potential to be tapped. You can explore that potential no matter what the circumstances.

Negative situations, such as handling a bully at your child's school or dealing with the aftermath of a car accident that wasn't your fault, can discourage even the most optimistic person. But when negative situations hit you—as they surely will sometimes—don't give up hope.

People who face chronic problems in their lives have to choose to be hopeful despite sometimes experiencing feelings of hopelessness. Linda Starnes sometimes struggles with all the tasks she must perform each day to care for her son Mac, who must use a wheelchair, breathe through a tube in his trachea and eat through a tube in his stomach. Parenting Mac and his older sister Emily, who suffers from a host of more subtle disabilities such as hyperactivity and impaired motor skills, "is the most exquisite joy and hardship at the same time," Starnes said. "If we didn't have our faith and know that there's a greater good in this, we would have crumbled a long time ago."

The hardship comes from dealing with her children's limitations day after day, but the joy comes from seeing

God's redemptive purpose unfold in the situation. When people first encounter Mac, they're likely to be uncomfortable, said Starnes. But after interacting with him, they learn how to be better explorers. "Mac teaches people that life is precious. He's able to push people to explore life in a different way when they're with him." Diane Anderson, director of the disabled people's ministry at the Starnes' church, said lessons people learn through interacting with children such as Mac and Emily are lessons that "we couldn't learn any other way. God's grace has to come into play in our weak spots."

If you strive to apply a sense of hope to the negative situations you encounter, you'll unearth lots of new ideas for dealing with them. And God will help you in the process. Remember, Jesus said, "`... all things are possible with God'" (Matt. 10:27).

Fortunately, many of the circumstances that color our lives aren't necessarily negative. But even when no problem is shouting for you to solve it, you can still be proactive about improving any situation. Exploring how you can be a blessing to those around you will reveal new ways of making circumstances even better than they are now. For example, if you start doing extra household chores to lift a burden from your spouse when he or she is stressed, you'll likely receive the gift of a loving response in gratitude. You may even initiate a fresh look at how chores are divided and how they might be done more efficiently all the time, making long-term changes for the better.

You can discover lots of new ideas—and help others discover them—if you strive to act out of an attitude of contribution, rather than merely consumption. For example, don't just attend worship services at your church; serve others by participating in one of its ministries. Or, if you enjoy visiting a particular park, consider how you might volunteer some spare time to help maintain it.

Exploration

Looking for humor

Humor often reveals new facets of situations that yield riches for explorers. When you find something funny, ask yourself why. Mulling over the reasons something amuses you helps you see an aspect of your life from a new perspective.

That's the great thing about humor—it changes your perspective, and often for the better. When people say others are taking themselves too seriously, they often mean that they're self-absorbed. An openness to laughing at yourself and the world around you fosters a healthy realization that the world is in God's hands, not yours. It also helps you make discoveries about the world, and yourself as well.

Some parents who enrolled their children in vacation Bible schools discovered that participating in the events alongside their children rather than just dropping their children off was surprisingly fun for them. At first, the parents admitted, they didn't expect to learn anything new about the Bible themselves, but the interesting and sometimes humorous experiences they had in the discussions and activities enlarged their perspectives. "It was really very fun ... " said George Galloway, the father of two young girls. "I went into it just expecting a family experience, but came out of it with even more than that. I learned a lot myself, which was a pleasant surprise."

People in a church theater troupe shared how the chance to act humorously on stage helped them discover more about their own God-given abilities. "I remember when I played the scarecrow in a production of *The Wizard of Oz* we did for youth, acting really goofy up there and seeing how the kids were really enjoying themselves, and that was rewarding for me," said troupe member Kevin Daniel. Experiences like that, he said, have helped him "to realize the uniqueness of how God has created me ... it's given me confidence."

There's certainly nothing wrong with indulging yourself

in humor. God does. "The One enthroned in heaven laughs..." (Ps. 2:4). God wants you to be joyful and has given you plenty to notice and enjoy. "Shout with joy to God, all the earth!" (Ps. 66:1). The unique character of all he has created—an amusing quirk in the personality of a friend or family member, a bird that strikes you as funny-looking—is something to celebrate.

Getting out in nature

God's creation has a unique way of speaking to the human spirit with divine insights. So take a few moments each day to explore nature.

When you step outside a building or car and into a forest or field, you're stepping outside the limits of environments created by humans and into an environment that reflects the master Creator's work. "For since the creation of the world God's invisible qualities—his eternal power and divine nature—have been clearly seen, being understood from what has been made, so that men are without excuse" (Rom. 1:20).

Many people have received great inspiration while exploring nature. In fact, the human creations that have been considered the greatest throughout history have profoundly reflected God's own creative work. Artists have created paintings that resonate in our spirits because they illustrate the intricacies of color and light God has made. Engineers have designed machines that are extraordinarily effective because they make good use of principles of physics God has set in motion.

As you explore, you'll be sure to discover many ideas you can develop further in the creative process.

CHAPTER FOUR

Inspiration

When God inspires you, he is breathing life into your mind and spirit, just as he breathed life into the bodies of the first humans he created. Gen. 2:7 records that, "The Lord God formed the man from the dust of the ground and breathed into his nostrils the breath of life, and the man became a living being." The word "inspire" literally means to infuse life into someone.

As descendents of those first humans—Adam and Eve—we're all infused with life from God at conception. The creative process of reproduction God set in motion many years ago continues to this day, resulting in multitudes of new humans born every day across the face of our planet. And all of us are made in God's image. "So God created man in his own image, in the image of God he created him; male and female he created them" (Gen. 1:27).

Connecting to God

God has bestowed the gift of creativity on everyone made in his image. "God blessed them and said to them, `Be fruitful...'" (Gen. 1:28). But we're not all able to use that gift equally well. Only those who access God's redemptive

A Creative Life

Spirit can be fully creative, fulfilling God's purposes.

The world we live in now is a fallen one, and all of it has been affected by sin. So life on earth is not as it was originally intended to be. "For the creation was subjected to frustration, not by its own choice, but by the will of the one who subjected it, in hope that the creation itself will be liberated from its bondage to decay and brought into the glorious freedom of the children of God. We know that the whole creation has been groaning as if in the pains of childbirth right up to the present time" (Rom. 8:21-22).

As God's creatures now inhabiting this fallen world, we're separated from God unless we establish a relationship with him through Christ, God incarnate. " ... all have sinned and fall short of the glory of God, and are justified freely by his grace through redemption that came by Christ Jesus" (Rom. 3:23-24). Many religions and philosophies focus on what people try to do themselves to relate to a distant God. Christianity is unique in that it focuses on what God does to relate to people—offering a direct connection to himself. Only those who possess that direct relationship can experience the power of the living God in their lives, enabling them to create works that are ultimately more profound than those who don't.

People connected to Christ, "in whom are hidden all the treasures of wisdom and knowledge" (Col. 2:3), are like the wise man who built his house on a rock that Jesus mentions in his parable in Matt. 7:24-27. Another man, representing those not connected to God, built his house on sand. Both could have been extraordinarily beautiful houses that demanded great creative talent to design. But only the one built on the rock—the foundation God intended—fully accomplished its purpose. When the house built with the flawed foundation was destroyed, the results of much creative effort were wasted.

As the apostle Paul mentions in Eph. 2:18, God will con-

Inspiration

nect you directly to himself through the Holy Spirit if you trust Christ. "For through him [Christ] we both have access to the Father by one Spirit." What better way to pursue a creative project than to be in contact with the source of all creativity?

Humbling yourself to trust

God entrusts his creative inspiration to people who he knows trust him. Those who have humbled themselves are ready to receive inspiration, because they recognize the value of God's ideas and are willing to accept them.

Since God has a purpose he wants fulfilled for every inspiration, he doesn't waste effort revealing creative ideas to those he knows are not prepared to receive them. Jesus explained that he often spoke in parables designed to inspire only those who had enough faith in God—rather than themselves—to understand. Speaking to his disciples, Jesus said, "The secret of the kingdom of God has been given to you. But to those on the outside everything is said in parables, so that, `they may be ever seeing but never perceiving, and ever hearing but never understanding ...'" (Mark 4:11-12). At first, that may strike you as cruel. But people only miss revelations when they're resisting them. Jesus affirms that God is always willing to inspire everyone as long as they are willing to humble themselves to trust him. "For whatever is hidden is meant to be disclosed, and whatever is concealed is meant to be brought out into the open. If anyone has ears to hear, let him hear" (Mark 4:22-23).

Women participating in community Bible studies discussed what a struggle it was for them to speak about their inspirations with others who didn't believe that the Bible truly is what it claims to be—God's revelation to humans on how they should relate to him and each other. In their daily lives, the women encountered people who claimed that any set of beliefs was equally valid and that a relativistic approach to life—trusting in whatever seemed right to them, rather than a universal God—could be creatively fulfilling. Those living relativistic lives were missing out on the creative insights and peace the women in the Bible studies were experiencing. "People can be put off and offended if they just hear Scripture quoted to them and they don't believe it," said Bible study member Fran Kashchy. "But if people are open to the possibility of a relationship with God like it's described in the Bible, he will work in their lives and they'll start to see the biblical principles lived out."

Another Bible study member, Diana Schick, said recognizing that absolute truth exists frees people from the limitations of looking just to themselves for inspiration. "Our world is set up with absolutes, but the postmodern thinking is that somehow in the spiritual realm, there are no absolutes, even though they exist in every other realm, such as math and science. Studying the Bible connects you to God's wisdom—eternal wisdom from the creator, not transitory wisdom from one part of creation, from one person in one place at one time. Man's thinking changes all the time, but the Bible is stable." By placing their trust in God, they opened themselves up to receive the most powerful and reliable inspiration available.

A woman caring for her elderly father trusted in God's wisdom as she sought to make decisions about how best to care for him. "I know that, while I love my dad, God loves him even more, and will always take care of him," said Becky Bishop, whose father, Gene Youngberg, was living in her home. "So if I pray about what to do and follow where God leads, things will work out." That humility and willingness to trust is the kind of attitude God is looking for in people he will inspire.

Consider whether you are truly open to receiving God's inspiration. Do you want to hear what God has to say? Are you willing to consider it? Maybe there are certain aspects of your life in which you may welcome inspiration, but others in which an innovative idea might be unwelcome, or even frightening. If there are any aspects of your life you haven't yet entrusted to God, try to surrender them to him in prayer, inviting him to transform them through his creative inspiration. "Submit yourselves, then, to God. Resist the devil, and he will flee from you. Come near to God and he will come near to you. ... Humble yourselves before the Lord, and he will lift you up" (James 4:7-8, 10).

Recognizing inspiration

Epiphanies—dramatic, watershed revelations in your life—are easy to notice. You probably can vividly remember the moment in childhood when you figured out how to ride a bicycle and took off without your training wheels attached. If you're married, you almost certainly can recall the time you sensed a certain person was the right one to become your spouse.

But life is full of many more subtle inspirations. God is willing to inspire you in innumerable ways every day, because he wants you to encounter him frequently. To be inspired is to encounter God in some way—to become aware of the divine presence that is always with you, but which you may not always notice, especially during particularly busy or mundane times in your life. The key to recognizing everyday inspiration from God is to invite him to speak to you in every situation, then expectantly listen for his voice.

Airline passengers and airport employees who visited airport chapels discovered that God was willing to meet with them during moments as mundane as taking a lunch break and as busy as rushing to catch a plane. Some took a few minutes to silently pray in the chapels; some picked up faith-based literature to read; some talked with airport chaplains about spiritual concerns. No matter how people used the chapels, God stood ready to meet with them "at their point of need," said airport chaplain Rev. Stan Esterline. Regularly seeking God's inspiration in the midst of life's routines helped airport employee Debi MacLean perform well in her job as a secretary there. "I've gotten into a routine where I pray in the chapel before work and at lunchtime ... the chapel is a blessing," she said.

No matter where you are, you can create a chapel in your spirit to invite God into your life. Take the time to ask God what ideas he'd like to reveal to you. The specific ways God inspires people are as numerous as the differences among people themselves. Since God created you, he knows how best to reach you with the creative inspiration he wants you to receive. You'll become aware of revelations on a regular basis once you scout them out. An interaction you witness between a parent and child in front of you in line at the grocery store can illustrate a Scripture verse and help you understand it more. A dream can give you ideas to solve a problem that's been perplexing you. As someone who writes about faith for a living, I've trained myself to look for divine inspiration in every situation I encounter—and I often find it, giving me an abundance of material for my stories.

Volunteers who helped others in their community through a grassroots coalition of churches said their service helped them recognize God's inspiration. As they banded together to provide people in need with emergency food, free furniture and rides to medical appointments, they were better able to understand the depths of God's love and apply it creatively to their lives. "Seeing the generosity of the donors and volunteers and the joy of the recipients, what I've witnessed truly is God's grace in action," said the coalition's vice president, Don Di Spirito. "It's very real and very significant. Just helping people in the most simple way, as Jesus did, cuts through all the sophisticated things that often can get in the way—the politics and all the divisions people can create. By serving people humbly as just one person to another, you get at the essence of what's really important—building relationships."

Inspiration from God resonates in your soul. It can be thrilling to experience; you may feel a surge of excitement, a wave of relief or simply a quiet sense of peace. But the key to discovering whether God is speaking to you isn't emotion. It's recognizing his voice.

A teen active in the Christian youth organization Young Life said the more time she spent seeking God's inspiration in prayer, the better she was able to recognize his voice. "It's really nice to be able to experience all the different ways Christ works in my life as I learn more about him and how to communicate with him," said Brittany Chow. "Some people have said to me, `How can you be so passionate about someone you can't see?' But I've found through Young Life that when I seek Christ, he becomes real and helps me become a more loving, more thoughtful and just better person."

God's goal when he communicates with you is to foster a relationship with you. The better you know God through that relationship, the better you can recognize that he is speaking to you. Jesus compared that dynamic to sheep that discern the right shepherd to follow. "[The shepherd's] sheep follow him because they know his voice. But they will never follow a stranger; in fact, they will run away from him because they do not recognize a stranger's voice. ... My sheep listen to my voice; I know them, and they follow me" (John 10:4-5, 27). The more time you spend praying, reading and absorbing Scripture, and worshipping Him, the more you'll recognize His voice. He will transform you during the process so you'll be able to hear and discern clearly.

Channeling creative energy

Throughout history, many people have channeled their creative energy in ways that bless themselves and others.

Scientists have formulated vaccines to protect multitudes from diseases. Musicians have composed songs to lift listeners' moods. Couples have borne children and invested their creativity into raising them to adults who contribute positively to society.

But many others—especially those who haven't sought God's guidance on how he intends them to use their creativity—have harmed themselves and others, either deliberately or unintentionally. Organized crime groups have devised clever strategies for thefts and murders. Politicians have concocted elaborate lies to cover up embarrassing facts they fear may keep them from getting elected. Authors have written entertaining plays that lead audiences astray by glorifying violence.

Your decisions about how to use your creativity can affect your life profoundly. "Those who live according to the sinful nature have their minds set on what that nature desires; but those who live in accordance with the [Holy] Spirit have their minds set on what the Spirit desires. The mind of the sinful man is death, but the mind controlled by the Spirit is life and peace ... " (Rom. 8:5-6).

Imagine that your mind is a large air duct. If it's filled with impurities, the air of inspiration flowing into it will be blocked somewhat by crud sticking to the sides, and the air of creativity flowing out of it won't be healthy. To clean your duct, heed 2 Cor. 10:5 ("We demolish arguments and every pretension that sets itself up against the knowledge of God, and we take captive every thought to make it obedient to Christ.") and Phil. 4:8 (" ... whatever is true, whatever is noble, whatever is right, whatever is pure, whatever is lovely, whatever is admirable—if anything is excellent or praiseworthy—think about such things.").

As you sift through new ideas that pop your mind, it's also helpful to pray about them. The Holy Spirit—whom Jesus promised in John 14:16 and 26 would act as a "counselor"—will give you discernment about whether a particular innovative thought is from God. This is important to confirm, since, at times, we can all be affected by evil. Those without a relationship with Christ are especially vulnerable to evil influences. "The god of this age has blinded the mind of unbelievers ..." (2 Cor. 4:4). But even Jesus was attacked by evil, and "Satan himself masquerades as angel of light" (2 Cor. 11:14).

An effective way to find out whether an idea is from God is to apply the advice in 1 John 4:1-3: "Dear friends, do not believe every spirit, but test the spirits to see whether they are from God, because many false prophets have gone out into the world. This is how you can recognize the Spirit of God: Every spirit that acknowledges that Jesus Christ has come in the flesh is from God, but every spirit that does not acknowledge Jesus is not from God."

Discerning the best from the good

Once you begin to recognize all the inspiration God can give you, you will experience the thrill of encountering him more. Each day will be filled with a greater sense of vibrancy than before. But you have a finite amount of resources such as time, energy, attention and money, and wise stewardship demands that you devote them to only the best ideas during the concentration stage of the creative process. So first, consider which of the many good creative ideas God has given you would be best to pursue.

Are you compelled to pursue particular ideas because you can't stop thinking about them? If so, God may be persuading you to act on those ideas. Even if that's the case, though, you also need to consider what's motivating you to embrace God's inspiration. Is your motivation to put your love for God into action? If so, the ideas are potentially worth pursuing. But if your motivation is primarily self-serving, such as simply to acquire more prestige or more money, you shouldn't invest your resources in the ideas. Many God-given ideas do lead to results that help the people who pursue them, but those results are byproducts of acting on the idea, not the motivation for doing so. A retired teacher may be inspired to start a tutoring business to help children after school. The business would have a good purpose, but is that project God's best plan for how the former teacher should invest her resources? If she's motivated to start a tutoring business primarily out of a desire for extra income or a way to avoid boredom in retirement—rather than a yearning to serve children—God is probably not calling her to pursue that idea. God's best for a person always involves putting love into action. If the retired teacher is compelled to start a tutoring business because she wants to help children, though, God may very well bless her financially or alleviate her boredom as byproducts of her service.

Apart from God, no one can do anything that will result in true fulfillment, no matter how good an idea might seem. If you're not certain about how you should respond to a particular creative idea, pray specifically about that idea, asking for guidance. God promises, "I will instruct you and teach you in the way you should go; I will counsel you and watch over you" (Ps. 32:8).

Recording your ideas

If you think of all the thoughts that enter your mind as raindrops falling from the sky, creative ideas from God could be seen as golden raindrops dropping to earth along with the plain ones. Those golden raindrops must be captured so their distinctive color doesn't wash out in puddles with the other rain, then evaporate and disappear into the air. That's why it's important to record the innovative ideas you receive—it's too easy to lose them if you don't.

An artist whose work was honored in a contest seeking images of Christ to celebrate the new millennium empha-

Inspiration

sized the importance of recording inspiration whenever it came to him. "Inspiration just hits me," Joseph Pisani said in his studio, surrounded by notebooks filled with sketches. Each time he got a new idea for how to flesh out a particular painting, he would add new details to an existing sketch or draw a new sketch to incorporate the idea into his emerging vision for the piece.

Pisani, who had enjoyed much success creating secular artwork—especially portraits of military and political leaders—over several decades, said he became more aware of God's inspiration through the process of working on his first religious painting. After recording the creative ideas he received for "The Taking of J.C." (which depicted Christ's betrayal in a modern-day Garden of Gethsemane), Pisani said inspiration for other religious paintings—such a portrayal of the Last Supper set in a modern subway station—came to him as quickly as if floodgates had been opened. "I think it was a message to me to do this [work on a religious painting]; sort of like a reminder," Pisani said. "I knew about God, but this was a way for him to remind me that this inspiration is coming from somewhere other than myself." Although Pisani hadn't set out to paint any religious works, he had heard God's call to do so and recorded the inspiration he received. It was through the process of recording that inspiration that he discovered even more creative ideas to broaden his career and deepen his relationship with God.

Soon after an innovative idea comes to you, strive to take a few moments to record it. Perhaps you could write it down; many people have found that recording their thoughts and feelings in journals helps them sort through their everyday experiences to discover great ideas. Perhaps you could record your idea on tape using audio or video equipment. Use whatever medium works best for you to capture the idea so you can access it later. While you record it, you may also consider what form your idea might take once it's fully expressed. For example, while you're driving, you may suddenly get an idea for how to prepare a creative dinner for friends who will be visiting your home in a few days. You could speak your thoughts into a tape recorder while in the car, but the dinner itself, of course, won't be on tape. Perhaps after listing ideas for ingredients you could add some notes to yourself on how you envision the dinner might look, smell and taste after it's been prepared.

Releasing the flavor of your ideas

Your tongue contains numerous taste buds, each programmed to enable you to experience the different flavors in the food you eat. But the taste buds aren't clustered all together in one small area; they're arranged at different points on your tongue's surface. As you eat an egg roll with hot sauce, for instance, the taste buds on the front of your tongue may register the sweetness of the cabbage and carrots inside, but you may not taste how hot the sauce is until it makes contact with the taste buds on the back of your tongue. It's only after you've taken a few moments to chew on the egg roll that you can discover all the flavors packed into it.

Each creative idea God gives you is like a morsel of food packed with many nuances of flavor for you to relish. If you take the time to ruminate on the inspiration you receive, you'll discover the full value of the gift God has given you.

When shepherds visited Jesus, Mary and Joseph in a manger shortly after Jesus' birth, they celebrated the inspiration angels had delivered to them shortly before—the realization that Jesus was God's Son. As Mary absorbed the full impact of what God was doing, she "treasured up all these things and pondered them in her heart" (Luke 2:19). Ps. 111:2 declares, "Great are the works of the Lord; they are pondered by all who delight in them."

God wants you to taste the full flavor of his inspiration so you can fully receive it, allowing it to accomplish its intended purpose in your life. The enormous potential of God's inspiration is evident in a passage from Hebrews that describes Scripture's power: "For the word of God is living and active. Sharper than any double-edged sword, it penetrates even to dividing soul and spirit, joints and marrow; it judges the thoughts and attitudes of the heart." (Heb. 4:12). When you're aware of the power God's inspiration can have in your life, you can develop a clear and compelling understanding of why it's important for you to pursue it. That motivation will help you later in the creative process, giving you the willpower to concentrate on your creative idea and the momentum to implement it. So savor the powerful flavors in all your creative ideas!

Stepping forward in faith

If you sense God calling you to pursue particular creative ideas, don't be afraid to step out in faith by deciding to act on them. Faith is a quality God highly prizes, and it's in faith that he hopes you'll respond to the inspiration he gives you.

Linda Wimpey, a homemaker who was inspired to help homeless people living in her county, decided while sitting at her kitchen table at home to begin a ministry to them. She began by delivering hot meals to people living in local motels, and over the years her ministry has grown to serve thousands of people annually, through the hot meals program and many others, such as those that offer job training, family enrichment and English and computer classes to people struggling with low incomes.

Wimpey's faith, which motivated her to respond to God's inspiration, is the key to her success, said Jim Callahan, who was helped by Wimpey and other volunteers from her ministry when he was homeless. In a daze from alcohol and drugs, Callahan told me, he heard Wimpey persistently knocking on the doors of the various motel rooms where he was staying whenever she made her rounds. "She kept knocking on my door," he recalled. "I didn't want to talk to anyone. It seemed like she would always catch me in a state of being completely out of it from drugs or in the throes of a hangover." But she was unfazed by his appearance, and kept stepping out in faith to pursue her idea of helping him. "She was just determined, and that will and that determination eventually won out," Callahan said. Wimpey and other volunteers "saved my life," he declared. "They loved me before I loved myself. They had faith in me."

As you prepare to concentrate on the creative ideas with which God has inspired you, claim the promise in Phil. 4:13 for yourself: "I can do everything through him who gives me strength."

CHAPTER FIVE

Concentration

Now that you know what God would like you to do, how do you do it? Responding to the creative inspiration you receive is vitally important. If you don't concentrate, life's demands can act like black holes for your innovative ideas, swallowing them up despite your best intentions. But you can see the fulfillment of your creative ideas by developing your concentration.

People sometimes think of creativity only in terms of exploration and inspiration. Moments of curiosity and discovery are fun, and it's thrilling to suddenly become aware of new ideas. But concentration? That can seem like too much work, or too boring to bother with when you're trying to be creative.

Concentration is actually a lot of fun, even though it might not seem so at first. Once you actually begin working with your creative ideas, you can start to experience the excitement of seeing them come to life before your eyes!

Dealing with emotions

Plunging an ice scraper into my car's windshield one wintry morning, I grew increasingly frustrated. It was demanding more time and effort than I would have liked to clear the ice, which sparkled beautifully in the sun, almost as if it was taunting me. Some hard blows broke the scraper, sending chips of plastic flying, and I groaned in dismay. But the same blows that broke the scraper also cracked a huge chunk of ice, sending it sliding off the car in defeat. I was thrilled to finally see a clear view through the windshield.

A creative idea may excite you as much as if it were sparkling in the sun. But when you start to tackle the hard work of pursuing it, you're bound to experience a myriad of emotions. The concentration process can elicit excitement, fear, frustration, satisfaction, disappointment, joy and every emotion in between.

Before plunging into a creative endeavor, ask God when he would like you to begin. This will help you avoid acting too soon out of excitement or procrastinating due to fear. Then entrust the results of your work to God, who will accomplish the purpose he intends for your creative idea. "And we know that in all things God works for the good of those who love him, who have been called according to his purpose" (Rom. 8:28).

God doesn't just hand you a map for your journey to pursue a creative idea—he serves as your guide, walking alongside you every step of the way. If you trust him with the details of your journey, you can experience the power of his presence, as the Hebrew people did on their exodus out of Egypt. "By day the Lord went ahead of them in a pillar of cloud to guide them on their way and by night in a pillar of fire to give them light, so they could travel by day or night. Neither the pillar of cloud by day nor the pillar of fire by night left its place in front of the people" (Exod. 13:21-22).

Knowing that God will be with you while you're working can give you the peace you need for the tasks ahead. Search and rescue team member Shawn McPherson, who I interviewed about his work responding to disasters worldwide, draws peace from God as he concentrates on helping victims. "It gives me a sense of calmness to perform my tasks to the best of my ability because I know that God is watching over me and the other members of my team," said McPherson, who traveled to Turkey twice in 1999 after its two deadly earthquakes, and to Oklahoma City after the 1995 bombing of an office building there claimed many lives.

In the face of such tragedy, McPherson strives to have a positive attitude—rooted in his faith in God's goodness—so he can concentrate on the work God has given him to do. "Things happen for a reason," he said. "You can try to rationalize them, or you can realize that sometimes God's perspective isn't our perspective. I always focus on the positive. There are many, many negative things that go on in the world—some caused by man, some by other things—but it's important to be positive. I don't have to understand the ultimate reason, but I do have to do my best to be faithful to do what it is that God wants me to do at the time. With every call, you go out with a clear mind and optimism in your heart."

God will enable you to concentrate on your creative work as you trust him, no matter what emotions you experience. "'Be strong, all you people ... and work. For I am with you,' declares the Lord Almighty. ... `my Spirit remains among you. Do not fear'" (Hag. 2:4-5). So make a decision to get started with your work. Then enjoy the process of working without worrying about the finished product. Remember that God's part is to bring about the results He desires from your work, and your part is simply to be faithful in doing it.

Taking inventory of your resources

Do you have what you need to pursue your idea? Jesus emphasized the importance of counting the cost of pursuing an innovative idea before acting on it. "Suppose one of you wants to build a tower. Will he not first sit down and estimate the cost to see if he has enough money to complete it? For if he lays the foundation and is not able to finish it, everyone who sees it will ridicule him, saying, `This fellow began to build and was not able to finish.'" (Luke 14:28-30).

Sometimes preparing to concentrate on a creative idea will be fairly simple—perhaps just organizing materials and blocking out some time in your schedule. Sometimes, though, God will ask you to make much more substantial changes in your life to prepare for your creative work. After my husband Russ and I had been married about one year, Russ told me he sensed God calling us to support a church his brother had started from scratch in a neighboring state. We had been attending the church each Sunday for a while, driving up and back each week, and contributing money to it as well. But to fully concentrate on the innovative idea Russ had to support the church by helping it grow, we needed to become more involved. That meant moving, which entailed many sacrifices for us. We had to spend a tremendous amount of money to move. We had to leave family and friends in our home state behind. I had to resign from a job I dearly loved that was too far away, and Russ had to take on a longer commute to his job. The process was very painful, but necessary to pursue that creative idea together.

Before you start concentrating on an innovative idea, ask God to reveal exactly what resources you need at your disposal to accomplish the work he wants you to undertake. Then take an inventory of your current resources by making a list of them, considering such topics as time, energy, money, materials, people to help and an environment in which to work. If you see deficits in your inventory, pray specifically about each void, asking God to equip you for the work ahead. Phil. 4:19 declares, "... my God will meet all your needs according to his glorious riches in Christ Jesus." Also pray for the strength to make the sacrifices you need to make to free up resources for your creative work. Perhaps you need to adjust your budget to make money available, or stop participating in a group that meets each week so you can carve out time to pursue your idea.

God may not always let you know everything you'll need for your creative efforts before you must begin acting on them. When he chooses only to give you enough information to take the next step in the concentration process, you may not know what else to ask for or how to pray for God's help. You can still pray for your needs during these times, trusting in the Holy Spirit to help you pray. "We do not know what we ought to pray for, but the Spirit himself intercedes for us with groans that words cannot express. And he who searches our hearts knows the mind of the Spirit, because the Spirit intercedes for the saints in accordance with God's will" (Rom. 8:26-27).

As you take stock of your resources and prepare to step into the work God has asked you to undertake, reminding yourself of the inspiration God has given you will help encourage you that all your work is worth the effort.

Choosing the important over the urgent

Dave Fried and Charlie Demers weren't likely candidates to spend six weeks bicycling across the United States. Dave was 63; Charlie was 50. Both men had full-time desk jobs, and faced many pressing responsibilities from those jobs, volunteer work, and full schedules of activities with family members and friends.

But God inspired the two to ride a tandem bike from Oceanside, California to Virginia Beach, Virginia in the spring of 2000, to raise money for charities and "leave the presence of Jesus with people we meet along our route by showing them unconditional love," said Fried, when I interviewed the friends for a story on their trip.

Concentrating on the creative idea God had given them meant putting many urgent things—other activities that seemed to shout for their attention—on hold. The important tasks at hand—activities that would help them fulfill their creative inspiration—were many. Fried and Demers devoted many hours to planning the trip over a two-year period, marking out a route, choosing stops at monasteries, searching for the right charities to support, creating an interactive Web site for people to check their progress during the ride, and more. During that time, the men logged more than 6,000 miles of bicycling time training for their approximately 3,240-mile trip. "It's very important to us to be attentive to the Spirit of God," Fried said. "Through prayer, we want to listen to what God has to say, to discern how God wants us to spend our time and how we should respond to the circumstances he brings our way. We live in such a controlling culture, that one of the most challenging things for us to do is acknowledge that it's God who is really in control of our lives."

During their journey, the men devoted the first hour of each day's bike ride to centering prayer, a form of silent prayer that focuses on preparing one's spirit to cooperate with God's leading. "One of the things that's key about centering prayer is humbling yourself to open yourself up to what the Holy Spirit wants for you," said Demers. "It's very humbling to see the Holy Spirit bring us everything we need to follow where God is leading."

The voice of the urgent often seems to be louder and more persistent than the voice of the important. Caving into pressure from urgent activities is easy to do when so many seem to follow you around, yapping at your heels like a small dog seeking attention—checking e-mail when a long list pops onscreen, running to the grocery store when you run out of something, sorting laundry piled up high, filling in for a volunteer who cancels at the last minute.

Sometimes you must deal with genuine emergencies. But most of the time, urgent activities aren't all that important.

And they can often wait until later.

Luke 10:39-42 records that when Jesus visited the home of two sisters—Mary and Martha—Mary "sat at the Lord's feet listening to what He said" while Martha "was distracted by all the preparations that had to made" for serving their guest. Feeling the pressure of the urgent, Martha said to Jesus, "'Lord, don't you care that my sister has left me to do the work by myself? Tell her to help me!'" But Jesus responded, "'Martha, Martha, ... you are worried and upset about many things, but only one thing is needed. Mary has chosen what is better, and it will not be taken away from her.'"

Strive to concentrate on important activities first, no matter how many urgent activities are pressing for your attention at a given time.

Dealing with interruptions

Interruptions can come in many forms—from an illness to an unexpected visitor dropping by—when you're trying to concentrate on a creative idea. Sometimes a particularly demanding season of life will push upon you constantly, making it a struggle to concentrate on anything for very long. Often, you can't control the circumstances you encounter, but you can control how you respond to them.

You can start by reminding yourself frequently of the creative inspiration God has given you, and why it's important to you to pursue that. Think of the passion God gave you for your innovative idea when you first received it. Don't let a single day go by without spending at least a few minutes concentrating on your creative idea, whether thinking about it or acting on it, because you never know how much time you'll have to pursue the idea.

An older man I knew had spent many years dreaming of visiting foreign countries with his family, but kept delaying trips due to distractions from his job. When he retired, he finally bought tickets for a tour of Europe, but died before he could take the trip. Death is the final interruption we all face with our creative work on earth, but there are plenty of other ways our creative ideas can slip away. An inventor who neglects regular work on his idea might see someone else develop and trademark it. A teacher who fails to tutor a student she had hoped to help might lose contact with the student when she moves on to another class.

"Let your eyes look straight ahead, fix your gaze directly before you. Make level paths for your feet and take only ways that are firm. Do not swerve to the right or to the left ... " (Prov. 4:25-27) advises. "Oh, sure," you might think. "That sounds good, but . . . " Granted, there will always be something that could stop you from concentrating on your creative work. You can meet those challenges effectively, however, by being proactive rather than reactive. You have the power to decide how you want to spend your time, and to enforce those decisions by saying "no" to interruptions that aren't important. The phone might ring, but you don't have to answer it. A festival may come and go, but the fun you have there will only lead to sorrow if you have to sacrifice your creative work to attend.

Sometimes interruptions are good. It's important to be flexible when God changes your circumstances and the Holy Spirit nudges you to respond accordingly. But it's just as important to remain focused on the task before you when interruptions come from other sources – as they frequently will.

Once you've dealt with interruptions from external circumstances, consider whether you ever interrupt yourself. If you do stop yourself from concentrating on a creative idea, there's usually an underlying reason why: fear. Cleaning out a closet when you'd meant to work on a speech or turning on the television when you should be practicing your soccer skills before a game aren't necessarily ways of avoiding your creative work. Often, they're ways of avoiding the pain you imagine you'll experience if you fail in your creative work. If you don't write that speech, you won't have to deliver it and risk people not receiving it well. If you don't get out on the soccer field to concentrate, you can excuse yourself if you don't play well in the upcoming game, since you didn't put out the extra effort.

Remember that fear is the opposite of faith, and if you choose faith by concentrating on your creative work even when you don't feel like it, God will help you in your work. Even acts of faith as small as the miniscule mustard seed can grow to tremendous proportions. Jesus said in Matt. 17:20-21, "I tell you the truth, if you have faith as small as a mustard seed, you can say to this mountain, `Move from here to there' and it will move. Nothing will be impossible for you."

So when interruptions come your way, ask God to give you "singleness of heart and action" to concentrate as he intends, just as he did for the Hebrew people mentioned in Jer. 32:39.

Planning for your best times

Not all interruptions are bad, however, and sometimes interruptions are a sign that you're trying to concentrate on an idea at the wrong time.

Staring at the computer screen, I gulped down some tea for a caffeine rush and tried to pull coherent thoughts out of my weary brain. Two o'clock in the afternoon was the time of day when I had the least amount of energy. But I was determined to try to cram in some work on a newspaper article. So I put my young daughter Honor down for an afternoon nap, fired up the computer and set out interview notes.

Slowly, the article began to take shape in my mind. But just as I typed my first sentence, I heard the click of Honor's bedroom doorknob turning.

"I'm not sleepy, Mommy," she announced, energetically skipping out. "I don't need a nap."

"But I need to write!" I thought desperately, my head pounding from too much caffeine.

"I need to go potty, Mommy," Honor informed me urgently. Unfortunately, waiting wouldn't work in that situation. We headed to the bathroom, and 10 minutes later I returned to steal a few precious moments of writing time while Honor colored a picture nearby. But wait ... what was that I was supposed to write down? All the ideas I'd had for how to organize the piece when I'd first tried to get started had disappeared.

The shrill ring of our telephone jolted me out of my mental fog, and I let the answering machine take the call, still hoping to accomplish something with my article. But as I listened to a friend leave a message, I realized that she needed to talk to me about something important. Finally, it began to sink in—this was not the right time to concentrate on the article.

My efforts to concentrate during the wrong time were essentially wasted, because they were unproductive. Investing my attention during the morning—when I had more energy, Honor was in preschool and friends didn't expect to reach me—would have reaped much greater results.

It's important to figure out what timing is best to concentrate on innovative ideas. "There is a time for everything, and a season for every activity under heaven ... " (Eccles. 3:1). A corporate manager might have creative ideas about how to better allocate his department's annual budget. But every Monday, he must participate in staff meetings that take nearly the entire day to discuss current client proposals. Tuesday through Friday, though, he has quiet time at his desk to focus on other tasks, and during the last few hours of the afternoon, phone calls and e-mails don't pour in as much as they do in the morning. He could commit to focusing on his budget ideas for at least one hour in the late afternoon, Tuesday through Friday.

You can discover what your best times to concentrate are—and why—by writing down how you spend your time for a few days, then studying the schedule to determine how you could have accomplished your tasks more effectively if you had scheduled your time differently.

Living in the present

Concentration demands living in the present, rather than the past or the future. Thinking too much about the past or the future is bound to distract you from the creative work you need to be doing now.

Members of the Washington Redskins football team shared with me how they relied on faith to play their best during the intense moments of their games. Resting on their laurels from the past or making cocky predictions about the future distracted them from their present work just as much as dwelling on a past loss to another team or worrying that an injury will end their careers.

Resisting the temptation to slack off because of a great past history of work was important to cornerback Darrell Green, who had already celebrated 17 seasons of victories with the team when I interviewed him. "The world says, 'Oh, you're doing great, so you should get a trophy and just rest on your laurels,'" he said. "But there's always more to learn, more to grow, to discover more and more of what God wants for me. I shouldn't just sit back and celebrate and quit. By continuing to be faithful, I can continue to grow."

Team chaplain Lee Corder said he often counsels players who are distracted by worries about the future. "Players know that 'NFL' can mean 'not for long,'" he said. "Any injury raises the question of what will happen in the future. These guys have reached the pinnacle of their dreams, and their careers are very tenuous after they've gotten injured."

After being sidelined for a while with a broken collarbone, wide receiver James Thrush said he discovered that

God has all time under his control. "Sometimes you can get caught up in thinking that you can be on the team forever, that whatever you want to happen will actually happen, but God's the one who's really in control. [Through his injury] God taught me not to take things for granted, but to trust him, and he'll be with me wherever I'm supposed to be."

God expects nothing less than the best when you're concentrating on your present work, said Ken Harvey, a former defensive lineman for the Redskins. "Everybody works hard during the game to do his best as God has called him to do," he said. "To give anything less than your best is to cheat God out of what he's given you."

Scripture emphasizes the importance of living in the present: " ... it is now that God favors what you do. ...Whatever your hand finds to do, do it with all your might ..." (Eccles. 9:7, 10).

Redeeming downtime

You might be surprised to discover exactly how much downtime you have tucked into the pockets of each day. Time spent waiting is a major chunk of that time—in line at a store, stopped at a traffic light, on hold during a phone call, sitting in a doctor's office before an appointment. Extra time might open up to you unexpectedly, if a business client calls to cancel a meeting at the last minute or your child's teacher reschedules a conference you'd been planning to attend.

Your downtime isn't likely to coincide with your best times for concentrating, but that's fine. When using your downtime to make some progress on a creative idea, the important thing is just to use it however you can, to make whatever progress you can, rather than letting that time go to waste.

You can redeem your downtime by making it productive. Try to carry some records of a creative idea with you wherever you go—perhaps some written notes or an audiotape of your thoughts so far on the idea—so you can add to them if you have some extra time to concentrate. Even when it's not practical to work on a creative idea, you can still use your downtime to think about it. Lying in bed before falling asleep, for instance, your mind may wander a lot. Disciplining your thoughts to focus only on a particular innovative idea would make wise use of that downtime. Multitasking by performing a mundane task such as sorting laundry while simultaneously thinking about a creative idea can also prove effective.

"Be very careful, then, how you live—not as unwise but as wise—making the most of every opportunity ... " exhorts Eph. 5:15-16.

Time management expert Ken Smith, who I interviewed for a feature story on the stewardship ministry he founded, emphasized the importance of making the most of every moment of time. "God is interested in how you spend your time," he said. "Time is the common denominator of life. Everything can be reduced to how you spend your time."

Additional inspiration has a way of showing up when you've got some free time. Perhaps, during a quiet moment of downtime, God will send you a new thought to build on an idea he has already given you.

Dealing with discouragement

There's nothing like the cold water of discouragement from others to put out the fire of excitement you have about pursuing your creative ideas. "Your idea sounds good, but it's not realistic," someone might say. Another might ask, "Nobody will appreciate your work, so why bother?" Still another might comment, "You must have an ulterior motive. I don't trust that you're doing this for the right reasons." Of course, someone might also simply tell you, "Your idea stinks."

When others who don't understand or appreciate the ideas God has given you dismiss or belittle the value of those ideas or the feasibility of pursuing them, it's easy for you to become discouraged. But you don't have to let discouragement interfere with your concentration.

Some students I interviewed about their efforts to reduce school violence by living out their faith mentioned how difficult it was for them to deal with the disrespectful behavior and comments of other students who didn't value peace as much as they did. When they got discouraged from witnessing fights in locker bays and taunting in classrooms despite their efforts to bring peace to their schools, they turned to God for encouragement.

The Holy Spirit helps them respond to discouragement by reminding them of the creative goal of peace he wants them to model, said high school student Ana Maria Skolnitsky. No matter whether the students are confronted by opposition to their peace efforts or some other type of confrontation, said Skolnitsky, they rely on the Holy Spirit for guidance in each situation. "By nature, we all just want to raise our fists and fight when someone makes us mad. That's human nature," she said. "I have been close to getting in fights once or twice, but I haven't, and I think it's because I remember biblical principles and they're greater than my anger. Plus God uses his Holy Spirit to put a little light on in my head and help me know what I shouldn't do."

A student at another high school, Cody Huston, said having a support network of people to turn to for accountability and encouragement helps him concentrate on fulfilling his goal of modeling a peaceful life for other teens. "As Christians, we have people in the church who we can go to if we need to talk. We have older, more mature brothers and sisters in Christ who will keep us accountable for our actions and behavior." An accountability partner, Huston said, also "models what a mature adult should act like," enabling him to "in turn, model appropriate behavior to my peers."

In the end, he said, concentrating on his creative idea of

working for peace does yield results, despite the discouragement that comes along the way. "Even one less person with a violent attitude greatly adds to the atmosphere of the school."

Heb. 12:1-3 describes how Christ himself endured discouragement and understands how difficult it can be, but concentrated on his work despite it and wants the faithful to concentrate as well. "Therefore, since we are surrounded by such a great cloud of witnesses, let us throw off everything that hinders and the sin that so easily entangles, and let us run with perseverance the race that has been marked out for us. Let us fix our eyes on Jesus, the author and perfecter of our faith, who for the joy set before him endured the cross, scorning its shame, and sat down at the right hand of the throne of God. Consider him who endured such opposition from sinful men, so that you will not grow weary and lose heart."

Often, however, other people can support you in valuable ways as you concentrate on your creative work. Seek out friends and family members who are willing to motivate you, encourage you, and offer you new perspectives and constructive criticism. Different people bring different strengths to contribute to creative efforts, and we all need each other. Fried and Demers drew great encouragement from their friendship during their cross-country bike ride. They said that the journey wouldn't have been nearly as fruitful had they traveled alone. Remember that, "As iron sharpens iron, so one man sharpens another" (Prov. 27:17).

Your work during the concentration part of the creative process is valuable not just for the personal growth you can gain from your experiences during that time. It will also pay many dividends once you present your creative work to the world.

CHAPTER SIX

Implementation

The world is waiting for your creative contributions, even without knowing that they exist. That's because God has designed a world that flourishes on the creativity of each part of it. Your creative work has great significance in the order of creation, since all of creation is nourished by the creativity released within it.

Embracing courage

Like many people, you may be a bit afraid to present your creative work to others, since you can't predict how they will react to it. But consider the loss people will suffer if they aren't able to experience your creative work in their lives. If you have an innovative plan to improve productivity at work, what will happen if you don't present that plan? If you've worked on a handmade present for a friend's birthday but decide not to give it to her, what encouragement will she miss?

I vividly recall the time I begged a high school English teacher not to make me read a paper I'd written, even though she told me she thought the paper's style was a great example of what she was trying to teach and that others would enjoy hearing it. The paper described an encounter I'd had with one of my favorite old movie stars, Ginger Rogers. But as much as I enjoyed old movies, I didn't think any of the other students would relate to them, and, worse, I imagined that they'd make fun of me for having an "uncool" cultural taste. My teacher read my paper to the class herself, as I squirmed in my chair. But afterward, instead of snickering, other students peppered me with lots of questions, telling me it was fascinating to hear about the glamorous things I'd described. And even if they hadn't reacted well to my creative effort, it still would have been worth reading it aloud if God had wanted me to do so. God is the only audience member whose opinion ultimately counts, and he always has a purpose in mind when he calls you to present a creative effort. Whether your creative work is something as simple as a school paper you've written or as complex as a building you've designed, God wants you to embrace the courage he gives so you can present it to others. As 2 Tim. 1:6-7 exhorts, " ... fan into flame the gift of God, which is in you ... For God did not give us a spirit of timidity, but a spirit of power, of love and of self-discipline."

A woman who was composing an anthem to celebrate her church's 125th anniversary shared how reticent she used to be when she thought about presenting her creative musical efforts to others. Linda Hannah could sing, play the organ and compose music well, but sometimes worried whether people would like the results of her work. When she needed encouragement to play or sing a song, she sometimes recalled what one of the church's former pastors had told her years before. "I remember Mr. Lukens [the former pastor] taught me that music is a gift from God, and as a gift from God, it must be used in service to others," she recalled. "Through the years during times when I haven't used it for awhile, I've felt empty. It was as if God was saying, `It's still there, so use it.'"

Implementation

Most often, people are afraid to implement their creative ideas for fear of rejection. But sometimes people are afraid of experiencing too much success when they unveil their creative efforts. If people love what they see, they'll expect more of it – and that means more hard work for those who present their innovations to the world. It's worth it, though. God especially wants those who are connected to him to deliver their creative work to the world, because their contributions help shine God's light into the darkness of a fallen world. " ... let your light shine before men, that they may see your good deeds and praise your Father in heaven" Jesus says in Matt. 5:16. Implementing your creative work is actually an act of worship, since you're offering a gift God has given you – your creativity – back to him to use in the world. No matter how other people react, God will be pleased that you used the creativity he have you. No matter what extra work might result, God will help you fulfill the requirements because you're faithfully doing what he asked of you.

You can trust God with the results of your creative work. People from congregations preparing for the dawn of the year 2000 discussed how they creatively prepared for what some thought might be a time of crisis (due to computer glitches when the new century arrived). But no matter how the various congregations prepared—such as by planning special New Year's Eve worship services or stockpiling a few supplies like food and batteries that community members might need—they embraced courage when they moved forward with their plans. "There was a lot of information [on what might happen] out there that raised panic in some circles of the public," said church member Wil Lepkowski. "But as Christians, we're called to trust God rather than fear." They decided that they would just do their best according to how they believe God had called them to act, and not be distracted by worrying about how their creative work would turn out.

Timing your presentation

You've been investing your creativity in a particular effort and are full of excitement about it. Maybe you're eager to share your creative work with others; maybe you're a bit intimidated about doing so, but still willing. So ... when do you present it?

First make sure your work has reached the stage at which it is complete enough to be effective. Col. 4:17 exhorts, "'See to it that you complete the work you have received in the Lord.'" Careful planning is the key to completing your work well.

People who decided that they wanted to distribute a copy of a Christian video to every home in their town—25,000 total copies—spent a long time preparing for their creative effort. One person got the idea for the project and suggested it to others in his church. Shortly thereafter, a core group of about a dozen people representing six area churches joined him to begin planning how to distribute the videos. Volunteers raised more than $90,000 to order the videos and nearly 200 volunteers placed the videos, some letters and response cards into gift bags. Then, 11 months after the planning officially began, more than 700 volunteers distributed the bags to each home in the town.

If the volunteers had not waited until they could obtain enough videos to deliver one to each home, people likely would have been upset that their neighbors received videos but they did not. If the videos had been delivered before explanation letters and response cards could be included, many people may not have watched them or let volunteers know what they thought of the videos. But the volunteers' careful preparation paid off. "The responses have generally been quite favorable," said Guy de Blank, who first suggested the effort.

Another important aspect of timing your creative presentation is discerning when people are ready to receive it.

Implementation

Volunteers working with grieving people in their community emphasized how important it was for them to be sensitive to whether it was the right time for them to talk with those who were grieving. Sometimes, they needed to wait a while, since the people they wanted to help weren't yet ready to talk about their loved ones who have passed away. "There is no timetable for grief, and a lot of people don't understand that, so a lot of our clients get pressure from their family members and friends to put on a happy face when they're not ready to yet," said volunteer Susan Keegan. "There are five stages of grief [shock, denial, anger, guilt and acceptance] that most people go through, but not everyone goes through them all, or all in the same order. [And] there are no shortcuts." Often, Keegan said, the volunteers' efforts to help the grieving people were more effective than the efforts of family members and friends, because the volunteers timed when best to present their help.

When trying to determine the best time to present your creative work, it will help immeasurably to pray for God to reveal that time to you. Keep in mind that, "There is a time for everything, and a season for every activity under heaven" (Eccles. 3:1).

Testing and validating your work

It's vitally important to test and validate your creative idea before fully implementing it, so you know that it's the best it can be. As you pray throughout the process, God will give you the discernment and peace you need to know when your creative work has reached its potential.

You can start by examining the details of how your creative idea might manifest once it's truly complete. That might involve activities such as making a list of the potential pros and cons that might occur after you introduce an innovative idea, or modeling how a physical creation might look or act. Modeling can be particularly useful for testing the feasibility of your work. A scientist might use a computer model to test how a particular medicine might affect a human kidney's function before actually giving it to people in clinical trials. An inventor might build a model of a toy to test whether its design manifests the way he thought it would.

God set forth detailed instructions in Gen. 6:14-16 for how he wanted Noah to build the ark, giving Noah a model of his creative plan from which to work. Even though Noah didn't need to test God's plan (since it was perfect), Noah surely derived confidence from seeing the ark modeled for him before he spent many years working to construct it.

People striving to use innovative teaching techniques in their Sunday school program tried various ways to present the same message to different children, according to how they could each best receive it. Children in the program rotated through different workshops to learn the same lessons—baking food, writing stories, singing songs, acting out dramatic skits, crafting art projects or exploring computer programs. The Sunday school leaders' efforts to test the feasibility of their curriculum in creative ways helped them effectively reach the children.

"There's a lot of variety, and that's why I like it," said then-11-year-old Sunday school student Fritz Reuter. "You get a different view of the lesson from each of the activities you do." Fritz's mother, Lexa Reuter, said both of her sons benefited from the teachers' willingness to test different ways of presenting their messages. "My kids have two different ways of learning, but they both are learning a lot in Sunday school," she said. "It's amazing how much they're learning from this multiple intelligence type approach that works with the different ways children are created, how each thinks best. The history and meaning of our faith is getting right down to their hearts. It's making a big impact on them. I think they're relating what they learn very well to their own lives and can see how God is working today."

If the response from students and parents hadn't been positive, Sunday school teachers would have tested other approaches to present the curriculum, said Susan Seehaver, the church's director of Christian education. The leaders' common goal, she said, was to "encourage children to participate in the creativity God has given them," however they could best do so.

Church members who operated community health ministries discussed how valuable it was for them to partner with a professional health care corporation in the area to validate their efforts to help community members with health issues. Although each congregation did the creative work of establishing and maintaining its own unique health ministry, the health care corporation gave them suggestions and provided resources to help them determine the best ways to implement their creative work. Through their partnerships with the corporation, the congregations were able to figure out whether their work was done well and would likely accomplish its intended purpose. They could determine the validity of their work and adjust it accordingly, such as by discarding an idea for an event they couldn't realistically produce or adding more depth to an existing program.

As you test and validate your creative work, strive to be patient through the process. "Perseverance must finish its work so that you may be mature and complete, not lacking anything," declares James 1:4. The results of all your hard work will be worth it. When your work is the best it can be, your creative contributions will be great.

Preparing for changes

As they're implemented, your creative efforts will inevitably change the circumstances of the situations into which they're introduced. You'll need to prepare for those changes by considering how various aspects of the situation will be affected. For example, a basketball coach can't introduce a new strategy into the game without somehow changing the actions of each team member and the outcome of the game itself.

Jesus emphasized the importance of implementing change fully rather than partially, so the changes will be effective. "No one tears a patch from a new garment and sews it on an old one. If he does, he will have torn the new garment, and the patch will not match the old. And no one pours new wine into old wineskins. If he does, the new wine will run out and the wineskins will be ruined. No, new wine must be poured into new wineskins" (Luke 5:36-38).

Your creative work may have to be implemented in phases, so it can be incorporated most effectively into an existing situation. The international ministry Habitat for Humanity, which helps provide homes for people who can't afford to buy or repair homes on their own, planned to build 18 new town houses in a particular town. As valuable as their creative plans were, however, Habitat volunteers couldn't start to build everything all at once. It took awhile to acquire the land, necessary building permits, funds and volunteer resources to even get started, and then logistics demanded that the project be implemented in two phases—constructing nine town houses at a time—rather than all at once.

Change can often be a gradual process. In 2 Cor. 12:20, Paul mentions his fear that the changes he and the Corinthian people would like to see in each other may not have been fully made by the time they meet. "For I am afraid that when I come I may not find you as I want you to be, and you may not find me as you want me to be," he writes. It can be challenging to wait for the change you hope your creative work will bring to fully take place. But when you ask God to shepherd you through the process of implementing your changes, he eventually will bring about transformation.

Some people recovering from homosexual lifestyles shared how the creative changes they were striving for were real, but gradual. God healed them over time, they said, being gentle with them even as he changed them profoundly. Susan Payne, who had spent 10 years living as a lesbian, said she was still undergoing change 17 years after leaving the lifestyle. Happily married with a then-5-year-old son, Payne said, "The process [of change] was real gradual, but God transformed me, and even now—17 years later—I'm still being transformed." Ray Enriquez (name changed at his request), who conducted clandestine homosexual affairs while he was a married father active in church, finally sought help after an affair he was having got exposed. "It's a process to change; it's not an overnight fix," he said. "But the healing is real, and the hope is real. You don't have to be gay. God will definitely work with you if you decide you want to change."

Payne said that God's gradual implementation of his creative changes in her life enabled her to grow to fully accept them. She said she came to realize that, "God did give us commandments and boundaries so that we wouldn't get hurt or hurt others. What a rich and abundant life God has for us if we just take him at his word. God has really helped me face my issues rather than just numbing myself to them like before. My sexual desire toward the same sex is gone. There is a way out, and that's through the person of Jesus Christ. I've discovered that, 2,000 years ago, Christ really did do that redemptive work to reconcile us to him to help us discover who we are—who he says we are and created us to be."

Enriquez said church members who aren't struggling with homosexuality themselves sometimes don't understand that healing is sometimes implemented gradually. "In some churches, there's sort of an unspoken demand that you've got to stop the behavior now or else. It really is a shame. With addictive behavior, sometimes it takes a while." He said he's grateful for God's patience in healing him of homosexual urges and helping his wife forgive and learn to trust him again. "It's a miracle," he said.

God will bring about the blessing he intends your creative work to have if you allow him to guide the process of implementing it. After all, he is in the business of transformation. "Therefore, if anyone is in Christ, he is a new creation; the old has gone, the new has come!" (2 Cor. 5:17).

Capturing people's attention

Your creative work could be among the most brilliant contributions the world has ever seen, but if people don't notice and fully receive your work, its purpose won't be fulfilled. That's why it's important to capture people's attention as you present the fruits of your creativity to them.

Just before God presented his intricate plans for the temple to the prophet Ezekiel, he showed him a man in a vision who captured his attention: "The man said to me, `Son of man, look with your eyes and hear with your ears and pay attention to everything I am going to show you ... " (Ezek. 40:4). Although Saul of Tarsus was "breathing out murderous threats" against Christians, God had a plan to transform his life. He appeared to Saul as Saul was walking toward Damascus, and that direct encounter with God certainly captured Saul's attention. " ... suddenly a light from heaven flashed around him. He fell to the ground and heard a voice say to him, `Saul, Saul, why do you persecute me?' `Who are you, Lord?' Saul asked. `I am Jesus, whom you are persecuting,' he replied" (Acts 9:3-5). When Saul got up from the ground, he was blind. God restored his sight through the disciple Ananias several days later, but only after Saul decided to pray. Saul, of course, later became Paul, who wrote many of the New Testament books.

People from a church with particularly dynamic volunteer projects emphasized how they needed to capture members' attention first to obtain the help they needed for all their creative service work—ranging from helping refugee families resettle in the United States to providing school supplies for poor children. "Although they recognize the needs around them, it is difficult for some people in this area to get involved," said Pat Seiler, the church's social action ministries coordinator. "They have busy lives, with long commutes and long work hours. But we try to give people an opportunity to be involved at whatever level they'd like and focusing on whatever interests they have. When people start to do things and see how other people are living, then their hearts are touched and they want to do more."

Members of a church theater company shared how a strong desire to capture audience members' attention kept them striving to be as creative as possible in their presentations. Company director Jack Kurtz, who writes most of its shows, said he keeps visions of audience reactions in mind throughout his creative process, even at the start of writing a new play. "I sit down and say, `What kind of theological and biblical understanding do I want to convey to people?' But that's just the start. It has to be embodied by real people living it out." Kurtz said he knows he has been effective with his creative projects if audience members tell him they think the action is realistic. He said one audience member told him, "'When the lights came up, I remembered it was a show.'"

By presenting messages through the medium of drama, company members are able to reach people who might not pay as much attention to the same message presented in a sermon, said member Neil Sampson. "Drama is a way to give voice to the message with an appeal to the emotions. That can be more effective for some people than just a factual presentation." The company's shows are "fun and they're comical, but they also portray a story effectively to get a point across," said member Rebecca Frye. "I think it's important to be fun to help people see things from a different perspective. They're more open to new ideas when you present them in a fun way." Humor is an important tool for company members to capture people's attention, said Kurtz. "I have an aversion to grim religious drama. ... Comedy in the show makes the drama more dramatic because of the context. There's no better way to be certain in what you've tried to do than when an audience laughs. Humor is a teaching tool. Jesus used humor to point out some of our natural human silly things we do."

The way in which you can best help people notice and receive your creative work depends upon the nature of that work and its intended audience. God will guide you to the methods that will be most effective.

Responding to feedback

You'll likely receive feedback on your creative work, and responding to it can help both you and others. Sometimes feedback will come in the form of praise for job well done; sometimes it will come in the form of suggestions for how to improve your work. Occasionally, feedback won't be constructive, but it's always worthwhile to listen to it. In 2 Cor. 6:11-13, Paul encourages the kind of open communication that fosters useful feedback: "We have spoken freely to you, Corinthians, and opened wide our hearts to you. ... As a fair exchange—I speak as to my children—open wide your hearts also."

A Christian coffeehouse had set up an advisory board made up of members of various local churches before even opening for the first time in a new town. The board members provided suggestions on how to establish and run the coffeehouse, and coffeehouse employees incorporated many of their suggestions, such as types of activities to schedule there. The coffeehouse, said advisory board member Pam Priester, "is looking to really offer something for everyone" in the community.

A church had provided sign language interpretation of its services and activities for the deaf people in its congregation for a while. But the deaf members still had to contend with a communication barrier, because hearing interpreters couldn't communicate as fluently with them as a person who was deaf could. Church leaders responded to the members' feedback by hiring a minister who was deaf himself, Mark Lowenstein. "They're deaf; I'm deaf. It breaks a barrier," he said. "Since I understand deaf people, I can give them a picture of God's plan. They listen with their eyes. There's more beauty of understanding God this way through a clear picture. It's more of a total communication."

That response greatly improved church members' relationships with God and each other. "All of a sudden, we are able to vividly understand everything without any need for an interpreter," said deaf member Cindi Cesone. "Our level of concentration has increased dramatically. ... This kind of a blessing has made an impact on our desire to mature in the knowledge and love of Christ." Another deaf member, Steve Williams, said he, too, was grateful for the response. "Now I can go up and discuss [something] with the preacher without a third party," he said. Deaf member Darrin Forshay appreciated the spiritual benefits. "With the new deaf minister, we can grow spiritually and spread God's message," he said. Deaf member Melanie Williams said the response to the needs of deaf people in the congregation is like, "a physical manifestation of God's love for me. ... The deaf ministry gives me a place where I am fully accepted for who I am, a deaf person and a Christian. This is just what Jesus does. He accepts each of us as we are and desires to help us become better people."

Responding to feedback you receive about your creative efforts will help continue those efforts as long as God intends, prolonging the benefits. You can fine-tune your work and grow in the process; others can more fully receive your creative contributions. Since God is always helping people grow in their relationships with him and each other, your creative work will continue to influence you and others even beyond the time you implement it. " ... he who began a good work in you will carry it on to completion until the day of Christ Jesus," declares Phil. 1:6.

The creative process itself—exploration, inspiration, concentration and implementation—will continue to play out in your life on an ongoing basis. As you use your creativity during the process, God will use his to continually mold you into the masterpiece he has designed you to be.

STUDY GUIDE

Becoming Fully Creative

The more you practice being creative, the more your life will become the masterpiece God designed it to be. You can start to experience a more creative life by applying the principles in this book through the discussion questions and the suggested activities listed here. Challenge yourself to think and pray about how you can immerse all aspects of your life in creativity. Remember: You can be creative at all times and in all situations!

You can use this guide either for your own personal study or for a small group study with others. However you use it, try to begin with prayer each time. Prayer will invite God to meet you in the midst of your study, making it come alive for you.

If you're meeting as part of a small group, you can do many of the activities together. Or, you can assign them as homework, then discuss them when you meet again. You may want to schedule a special meeting at the end of your session to give each group member an opportunity to share a creative project with others in the group. My husband and I were glad we did so when leading a Bible study on creativity. What fun it was to see how the people in our group

– with diverse personalities and backgrounds – each put his or her creativity to use in unique ways.

Enjoy!

Chapter One: God the Creator

"Knowing the master Creator"

<u>Discussion question:</u> What would you like to know about God that you don't already know?

<u>Discussion question:</u> How does God's mystery entice you to seek him more?

<u>Activity:</u> Write God a letter, asking him as many questions as you'd like. Then present the letter to him in prayer, including some time for quiet reflection afterward to listen for his voice if he chooses to speak to your spirit then.

"God is loving"

<u>Discussion question:</u> How has God demonstrated his love in your life lately?

<u>Discussion question:</u> Think of a challenging situation in your life right now—perhaps a strained relationship with someone, or circumstances that are discouraging you. What are some ways you can rely more on God's love to help you creatively approach that situation?

<u>Activity:</u> Draw a picture of yourself, illustrating a part of your appearance or personality that you don't particularly like. Then add an illustration of Jesus into your picture, embracing you with love exactly as you are.

"God is purposeful"

<u>Discussion question:</u> What are some of the purposes you

believe God has for your life?

Discussion question: How have you experienced God working in your life lately to connect you to others? How can you work together with them to live creatively for God in a particular situation?

Activity: Read Psalm 138:8 and Psalm 139:1-16 aloud. Afterward, write a list of some of the ways it illustrates how God is purposeful when he creates human beings. Then list a few ways it helps you understand more about his purpose for your own life.

"God is infinite"
Discussion question: How does the knowledge that God's power is infinite give you confidence in your life?

Discussion question: Think of a challenging situation in your life right now. How can you rely more on God's infinite wisdom to help you deal with it creatively?

Activity: Go outside on a clear night to view the stars in the sky. Try to associate each star with a blessing from God, big or small. Then thank him for all he provides for you out of his infinite supply of blessings.

"God is dynamic"
Discussion question: What are some natural changes you've observed lately that you appreciate, and why?

Discussion question: Which aspect of your life would you most like God to transform, and how can you invite him to do so more?

Activity: Choose a simple science or cooking project to do

to observe how chemicals change when mixed together in different ways. For example, you could try mixing baking soda with vinegar.

"God is emotional"
Discussion question: When you ponder how much God cares about his creation—including you—how does that draw you closer to him?

Discussion question: As Jesus, God experienced every emotion you've ever felt—from sorrow to joy. How does that knowledge help you appreciate your own emotions?

Activity: Imagine that you're in the middle of a situation that's perplexing you right now and consider how Jesus might approach that situation. Playing the role of Jesus, act out emotions you imagine he might experience as he deals with the situation.

Chapter Two: Made in God's Image to be Creative

"Creatures meant to create"
Discussion question: What are some ways you can practice better stewardship of God's creation?

Discussion question: How have you recently experienced the connections between the spiritual, mental and physical aspects of yourself?

Activity: Plant a flower, vegetable or fruit of your choice. As you take care of it and watch it grow, pray that God will help you grow healthier spiritually, mentally and physically.

"Building creativity through spiritual intimacy"

<u>Discussion question:</u> What spiritual discipline do you practice the least, and how can you incorporate it into your life more?

<u>Discussion question:</u> When have you been especially aware of God's presence with you recently?

<u>Activity:</u> Add 15 extra minutes of prayer into your day for one week and use it to pray specifically for grace to start living more creatively.

"Building creativity through mental attitudes"

<u>Discussion question:</u> How can you put a little vacation into your day today without necessarily taking a trip?

<u>Discussion question:</u> What is cluttering your life, and how can you eliminate it to free yourself for more meaningful pursuits?

<u>Activity:</u> Think of an attitude you would like to embrace more—such as curiosity or courage. For one day, decide to act as if you already had the attitude, and notice the difference in your day. That night, pray for God's grace to help you live more days with that attitude.

"Building creativity through physical care"

<u>Discussion question:</u> What are some ways in which you would like to start taking better care of your body?

<u>Discussion question:</u> How has your body served you well during a recent creative effort?

<u>Activity:</u> Choose one lifestyle change to make to improve your physical health, then tell a friend or family member

your plan and ask him or her to help you stick to it by encouraging you and holding you accountable.

"Getting ready for adventure"
Discussion question: What are some of your unique spiritual, mental and physical gifts?

Discussion question: How can you use your gifts more fully to serve God?

Activity: Imagine that you're planning a trip to heaven. Draw a picture of a suitcase on a piece of paper, then "pack" it for your trip by listing several spiritual, mental and physical qualities you would like to take with you.

Chapter Three: Exploration

"Becoming an explorer"
Discussion question: How have your life's circumstances discouraged you from exploring in the past, and how can you begin to overcome those circumstances by exploring more right where you are in life?

Discussion question: What are some topics you would like to explore, and why?

Activity: Schedule an outing sometime soon to a nearby place you enjoy—a park, a restaurant, any place at all. Sit there for half an hour, playing close attention to your surroundings and making a list of every interesting thing you notice.

"Developing a sense of wonder"
Discussion question: Think of a characteristic that you par-

ticularly admire about God—his love or his wisdom, for instance. How is that characteristic reflected in how God is currently working in your life?

Discussion question: What was one thing you noticed lately that intrigued you, and why?

Activity: Study the intricacies of how God has designed a part of nature by researching your subject in search of new facts about it. For example, if you have a pet, you may choose to research that particular type of animal. If you enjoy stargazing, you might research a specific constellation.

"Relinquishing the status quo"
Discussion question: Which aspects of your life would you be most afraid to see undergo changes, and why?

Discussion question: Consider what changes you would like to see happen in your life. What steps might you take to begin incorporating them gradually in your life?

Activity: Envision a situation in your life that is stagnant. Symbolically place it in your hands, then lift your hands heavenward, praying for God to take control of the situation and make it more dynamic in ways that he chooses.

"Embracing forgiveness"
Discussion question: What hurts have you suffered in the past that continue to haunt you?

Discussion question: How did you feel after you made a recent mistake? Your mistake may have hurt God, but didn't reduce the level of God's love for you. How does the knowledge that God always stands ready to forgive you free you to move forward with your life?

Activity: Contact someone who has hurt you to let that person know you have forgiven him or her. Pray for God to bring peace about the situation into your spirit and the spirit of the person to whom you are extending forgiveness. If possible, visit the person you are forgiving so you can be face-to-face when you talk. If the person is deceased, write a letter telling him or her that you forgive. Even though you won't be able to mail it, you will still have expressed your forgiveness.

"Finding the `right' way to do things"
Discussion question: What pressures have you experienced lately from others to do things differently from the ways God seems to be leading you to do them?

Discussion question: What fears are blocking you from following God's lead in those situations?

Activity: In front of a mirror, practice telling someone that you have chosen a different course of action from what they were expecting in a certain situation. Work on building your courage to actually tell that person face-to-face, in a firm yet loving manner.

"Placing margins in your life"
Discussion question: What steps can you take to create some more free time in your life?

Discussion question: How did a recent block of free time help you explore your surroundings more?

Activity: Refrain from work and attend worship on the Sabbath. At night, record how you benefited from the day.

"Listening enthusiastically"
<u>Discussion question:</u> Have you heard from God lately? If so, how did you sense him speaking to you?

<u>Discussion question:</u> How could you listen more closely for God's voice? How could you pay more attention when another person is speaking to you?

<u>Activity:</u> Interview a few friends or family members, asking them questions about subjects that interest you—such as how they met their spouses, what their favorite food is and why, or what they consider to be one of their most embarrassing moments.

"Trying new things"
<u>Discussion question:</u> What are some new experiences you would like to pursue, and why?

<u>Discussion question:</u> What has stopped you from trying new things in the past, and how can you overcome those obstacles?

<u>Activity:</u> Choose one new experience you've been wanting to pursue for a while, and schedule a time to engage in it soon.

"Looking for potential"
<u>Discussion question:</u> Do you feel overwhelmed or even trapped by a negative situation right now? How could you rely on God to help you see the potential for that situation to improve?

<u>Discussion question:</u> How can you proactively improve a situation that's not necessarily negative, but still could get better?

Activity: Contribute your volunteer services to an organization whose work you appreciate and notice how your efforts help the organization reach more of its potential.

"Looking for humor"
Discussion question: When you laughed about something recently, what was it that made it so funny to you? Did the humor in the situation help you see new facets of it that you wouldn't have noticed otherwise?

Discussion question: Do you ever stifle your laughter when something strikes you as funny? If so, why? How could you start to enjoy humorous moments more?

Activity: Go ahead and indulge yourself in some humor. First, seek out humor, perhaps by reading the comics in your local newspaper or renting a comedy video. Then, create some humor, perhaps by telling a joke or swapping stories with a friend about silly moments from each other's lives.

"Getting out in nature"
Discussion question: How can you change your schedule and your lifestyle to spend more time outdoors?

Discussion question: How does being out in nature help you sense God's presence with you?

Activity: Get out there! Plan to spend at least half an hour outdoors sometime soon. The place can be anywhere—even your backyard. While you're there, study your surroundings, looking for details that might intrigue you. Spend some of your time in silent prayer, thanking God for creating that environment and asking him to speak to you through it.

Chapter Four: Inspiration

"Connecting to God"
Discussion question: Are you connected to God through a relationship with Jesus Christ? If so, how have you experienced God fulfilling his intended purposes for your creative efforts?

Discussion question: How can you more fully consecrate your creative efforts to God?

Activity: Invite God to participate more in your life by offering each aspect of it to him in prayer.

"Humbling yourself to trust"
Discussion question: Think of a situation that is perplexing you right now. How can you clear out your own assumptions about it to make room for hearing God's guidance for the situation?

Discussion question: What are some recent times when you have been tempted to rely just on yourself rather than on God? When facing similar situations in the future, how could you rely more on God?

Activity: Purposely delay making a decision about something until you've prayed about it and promised God that you'll act according to his desires. Then make the decision only after God has given you confidence and peace about it.

"Recognizing inspiration"
Discussion question: Do you sense God's presence with you regularly, or does he seem distant?

Discussion question: Recall a particularly rewarding time

you received inspiration. How did that experience draw you closer to God?

Activity: Spend a day praying as frequently as you can, turning thoughts into prayers throughout the day as if engaging in an ongoing conversation with God. Include some regular time for silence as well, to listen for God's replies if he chooses to speak to your spirit then.

"Channeling creative energy"
Discussion question: What are some positive ways that you've channeled your creativity in the past? What are some ways you've channeled your creativity that you regret?

Discussion question: Think of a creative idea you've received recently. Would you be honoring God if you were to pursue it?

Activity: In prayer, repent of any sins that may be blocking you from hearing and following God's guidance in your life, and ask God to help you resist any evil that might seek to influence your decisions.

"Discerning the best from the good"
Discussion question: Out of the many good ideas for creative projects that you could potentially pursue, which interest you the most?

Discussion question: Why do those particular ideas strike you as the best ones? If you were to pursue them, what would be your motivation for doing so?

Activity: List the pros and cons of several ideas for creative projects that appeal to you.

"Recording your ideas"
<u>Discussion question:</u> How did you feel the last time an inspiration slipped away from you because you didn't record it?

<u>Discussion question:</u> How did your records of another inspiration help you pursue that idea later on?

<u>Activity:</u> Resolve to record future ideas that come to you, then practice by carrying a notebook around with you for one full day, recording every idea for a creative effort that comes your way.

"Releasing the flavor of your ideas"
<u>Discussion question:</u> As you've pondered a recent idea, what more have you discovered about it?

<u>Discussion question:</u> How does thinking about the ideas God gives you help you appreciate God's infinite wisdom?

<u>Activity:</u> Heat a cup of water, then drop a tea bag into it. After just a few seconds, remove the bag and drink a few sips of the liquid. Then place the bag back inside the liquid and let it remain there for several minutes. Take another sip, and notice the difference in flavor once the tea has been released more into the water.

"Stepping forward in faith"
<u>Discussion question:</u> Has God given you an idea you haven't acted upon yet, but know that you should? What idea is it?

<u>Discussion question:</u> What initial steps can you take to pursue an idea on which God is calling you to concentrate?

<u>Activity:</u> Step forward! Start concentrating on a creative idea God has given you, even if you feel afraid to do so at

first. God will reward your obedience with all the help you need along the way.

Chapter Five: Concentration

"Dealing with emotions"
<u>Discussion question:</u> What types of emotions have been interfering with your ability to concentrate lately? How do you think God could help you overcome those emotions so you can concentrate better?

<u>Discussion question:</u> How have your emotions helped motivate you to pursue a creative effort in the past?

<u>Activity:</u> Pray for God's peace to reign in your mind as you try to concentrate on your creative work.

"Taking inventory of your resources"
<u>Discussion question:</u> Do you have the resources necessary to do the creative work you're planning?

<u>Discussion question:</u> If you don't have all you need to concentrate on your creative efforts, how can you obtain those resources?

<u>Activity:</u> Envision the form a creative idea you have might take once it's complete. Make a list of everything you anticipate needing to work on it, and pray for God to provide all that, plus whatever you can't anticipate.

"Choosing the important over the urgent"
<u>Discussion question:</u> What are some activities that shout for your attention on a regular basis, and how can you minimize their power to distract you?

Discussion question: How can you rearrange your schedule to devote more time to important activities and less time to urgent ones?

Activity: Block out an hour to concentrate on your creative work no matter what. Choose a busy place in which to work and a time during which many other matters need your attention, so you can practice concentrating in the midst of potential distractions.

"Dealing with interruptions"
Discussion question: What are some ways you can prevent unexpected circumstances from interrupting you?

Discussion question: What fears sometimes cause you to interrupt yourself?

Activity: The next time something or someone threatens to interrupt you, firmly yet respectfully decline to take your attention away from your creative work during the time you have scheduled to do it.

"Planning for your best times"
Discussion question: When have you recently tried to concentrate on a creative effort at a bad time, and what happened as a result?

Discussion question: What time of day is best for you to concentrate, and why?

Activity: Rearrange your schedule to carve out more opportunities to concentrate on your creative work during the times that are optimal for you.

"Living in the present"
Discussion question: How have thoughts about your past or your future distracted you from concentrating on your present activities?

Discussion question: How can you concentrate more on living one day at a time, drawing strength from God's presence with you no matter what you're doing?

Activity: Engage in a recreational activity of some kind – perhaps a sport or an art project – while trying to pay close attention to the activity. Afterward, reflect on how many times you let your mind wander.

"Redeeming downtime"
Discussion question: If you could have 25 hours in every day rather than 24, how would you use the extra hour?

Discussion question: What steps can you take to prepare yourself to more effectively use downtime as you encounter it?

Activity: Make a list of all the pockets of downtime you can remember from your schedule over the past few days. Estimate how much total time it all adds up to, and consider how you might use that same amount of time over the next few days in more creative ways.

"Dealing with discouragement"
Discussion question: When someone recently belittled an idea of yours or expressed doubt about how it would turn out, what did that person say or do, and why did that experience discourage you?

Discussion question: How could you have responded better

to that experience so that it wouldn't have sapped your enthusiasm?

Activity: Study a crucifix or some other illustration of Jesus on the cross. Imagine the depth of pain he endured while doing his great creative work of redeeming the world. In prayer, ask him to give you strength to overcome discouragement.

Chapter Six: Implementation

"Embracing courage"
Discussion question: What fears do you have about presenting your creative efforts to others? How can you rely on God to help you overcome them?

Discussion question: What blessings will people miss if you don't present your creative work to them?

Activity: Enact the scenario of you presenting your creative work to another person. Play the role of yourself and ask a friend to play the other person. Act out different things you imagine might happen when you present your creative work. When you're finished, assure each other that no matter what actually does happen, your creative work is worthwhile.

"Timing your presentation"
Discussion question: Is your creative work complete enough to be effective, or do you think you should wait a while before presenting it?

Discussion question: How can you best plan the logistics of delivering your creative work?

Activity: Study the intended audience for your creative work to determine whether people are ready to receive it.

"Testing and validating your work"
Discussion question: How would testing a particular project help you determine its feasibility?

Discussion question: How could you best validate a particular creative project?

Activity: Design a way to test one of your creative projects.

"Preparing for changes"
Discussion question: How do you anticipate that your creative efforts will change the circumstances of situations into which they're introduced?

Discussion question: How can you best plan to implement your creative work gradually?

Activity: Draw a diagram that represents the connections between all the different aspects of the situation into which you plan to introduce your creative work.

"Capturing people's attention"
Discussion question: To whom is God calling you to present your work, and why?

Discussion question: What needs does your audience have, and how can you speak to those needs as you present your work?

Activity: Write a plan detailing how you think you can best capture people's attention when you implement one of your creative efforts.

"Responding to feedback"
Discussion question: Is feedback on your creative work important to you? Why or why not?

Discussion question: How can you work to build relationships with people who give you feedback on your creative work?

Activity: Don't just wait for feedback; ask for it. Engage people in conversations about your creative work, and respond to what they say as God leads you.

Printed in the United States
6108